ADMINISTRATIVE ETHICS AND DEVELOPMENT ADMINISTRATION

Jean-Claude Garcia-Zamor

D0912386

University Press of America,® Inc.
Lanham · New York · Oxford

Copyright © 2001 by
University Press of America,® Inc.
4720 Boston Way
Lanham, Maryland 20706
UPA Acquisitions Department (301) 459-3366

12 Hid's Copse Rd.
Cumnor Hill, Oxford OX2 9JJ

ISBN 0-7618-2184-8 (pbk. : alk. paper)

⊖™ The paper used in this publication meets the minimum
requirements of American National Standard for Information
Sciences—Permanence of Paper for Printed Library Materials,
ANSI Z39.48—1984

To my inamorata
Patricia E. Soper

and

my daughter
Christabel McEwan Garcia-Zamor

CONTENTS

LIST OF TABLES

ACKNOWLEDGMENTS

I am grateful to the various deans I have had since I joined FIU in the Spring of 1990: Allan Rosenbaum, presently the Director of FIU Institute of Public Management; Mark B. Rosenberg, presently the Provost and Executive Vice President for Academic Affairs of the University; and Ronald M. Berkman, the present Dean of the College of Health and Urban Affairs. Each one of them had giving me the time and the opportunity for starting new academic activities.

A good friend and colleague, Ferrel Heady of the University of New Mexico, spent valuable time reading over my first draft, suggesting changes and sending some valuable comments. I am deeply indebted to him.

I have also incurred a number of debts of gratitude in preparing the manuscript. Five of my FIU graduate students have helped with library or Internet research: Kathy A. Ashby, Irene S. Cabral, Tereena L. Joubert, Carlos M. Zepeda, and Ellen A. Plissner. In addition, Elyse A Rosenberg did some library and Internet research for me while taking an independent research seminar with me during her senior year at FIU. I am especially grateful to Rosa Davis, a Ph.D. student in the School of Policy and Management. She helped me in the preparation of the final draft after the manuscript was completed. Her task was very arduous and she demonstrated patience, great skill and dedication in accomplishing it.

Finally, I dedicate this book to two individuals very dear to me: Patricia E. Soper who have been inspiring me since we met in May 1991, and my daughter Christabel. Both have given me support and encouragement in the various academic activities I have recently undertaken.

Jean-Claude Garcia-Zamor

INTRODUCTION

Most critical issues of government and public administration involve ethical dilemmas. Policy decisions by bureaucrats in both the industrialized countries and the developing ones are often made in the context of conflicting ethical and moral issues. This book looks at administrative ethics and development administration in a comparative perspective, reviewing different aspects of the two processes and relating the developmental process with ethics. These two conceptual processes are vital for the survival of effective and democratic civil services.

Administrative ethics is a system of rules enforced by such administrative sanctions as demotion and firing, as opposed to rules enforced by such civil or criminal sanctions as monetary penalties or imprisonment. This view of administrative ethics has at times been broadened, from a system of enforceable rules, to a coherent system of rules and principles that combine to create an environment that fosters ethical behavior.

Development administration is the human participation in the national development of a country. "National development" here does not refer solely to economic development, but also encompasses the over-all process of creating the concepts, symbols, and institutions that give a philosophy, structure and identity to a modern nation-state. Effective institutions are universally regarded as playing a strategic role in the development of a country. Effective public-sector institutions allow governments to perform two important functions: a) elaborate appropriate development goals and policies; and b) implement them in such a way that the goals are achieved. The book illustrates how the weakness of public-sector institutions in developing countries has deprived these nations of the capability to perform these functions and how sound administrative ethics can strengthen these institutions. Although each country might have its own understanding of administrative ethics, there is a growing consensus on ethical norms, standards and codes of conducts across regions and cultures.

The terms morality and ethics are interchangeable but many ethical violations are not necessarily unlawful. They occur during the performance of routine tasks by public servants every where. Such hard-core corruption as theft and bribery are clearly criminal cases. However, when ethics is being considered, the issues that are debated involve morality, human rights, and values. Unfortunately, too many contemporary public servants are primarily concerned with walking the narrow line that keeps them out of legal troubles. In a different time, this concern was addressed in a different way by Edmund Burke when he opposed British suppression of the American Revolution: "It is not what a lawyer tells me I may do, but what humanity, reason, and justice tell me I ought to do." Although good laws are indispensable for a working democracy, they are of no use without ethics—without the individual being willing to adhere to these laws. The democratic nations do have many public servants with good character but sometimes they are voices in the wilderness when important decisions are being made by government officials preoccupied only with the politics of the moment. In these cases, the proper functioning of a democratic system is endangered by such deterioration of ethics because democracy is based on the assumption that the government and the public service are basically honest.

The principle of justice, which requires a moral basis for discerning right from wrong, used to be a dominant virtue in Western culture. Similarly, ethics were woven in the very fabric of Western society. But unlike other Western values, time and space dictate the parameters of ethical boundaries. The four chapters in Parts III and IV that deal with the cases of Latin America and Africa clearly indicate how cultural contexts often determine the rightness or the wrongfulness of an administrative action.

The book establishes a clear and vital connection between administrative ethics, successful modern economies, and good democratic governments in both the industrialized and the developing countries.

PART I

ETHICS AND DEVELOPMENT IN AN INTERNATIONAL COMPARATIVE FRAMEWORK

The three chapters of Part I discuss the ethical situation that exist in the bureaucracies of small and developing countries. The chapters look at the inner working of the bureaucracies and concentrate on the problems, dilemmas, and conflicts that characterize them. One of the issues addressed is how to develop ethical standards in bureaucratic practices in environments marked by poverty and other urgent basic needs.

Chapter one introduces the concept of "micro-bureaucracies" in which a type of informal clique or faction of officials organize themselves to promote political or administrative objectives. The former category, which sometimes aims at the overthrow or transformation of an existing regime, is composed of policrats, whereas those drawn to the latter function are the technocrats. The former must often perform work in secrecy, whereas the latter can be more openly active. The chapter also points out the role of micro-bureaucracies in development administration and suggests how the theories advanced in the chapter could be tested in developing countries' political systems.

The main assumption of chapter two is that small and island states' bureaucracies find it quite difficult to develop and apply administrative ethics. The chapter has four parts. In the first one, a profile of the small and island states is presented and several definitions of "smallness" are reviewed. The 26 smallest islands and smallest states of the world — all with a territorial size of less than 1,000 square miles — and all fully independent nations, are analyzed in the study. Several tables are used to compare their territorial sizes, populations, cultural heritages, literacy rates, life expectancies at birth, and international links. World Bank data are used to classify their economies by income and region, and United Nations data are used to establish the Human Development Index (HDI) of each state. The second part of the chapter discusses the general characteristics of the bureaucracies of small and island states. Part three reviews several ethical theories that are usually translated into codes of ethics for public employees in many countries. It discusses why their application in small and island states is difficult. Finally, in part four, information obtained from the Internet is used to analyze the level of application of administrative ethics in the small and island states. The chapter ends with a discussion of how massive new technology being presently developed might affect the future of administrative ethics in the small and island states.

In the field of public administration, conflicts are viewed as inevitable due to many differences among people who may have dissimilar points of view and/or goals. Thus, total elimination of conflicts is not a reasonable expectation, nor would it be very healthy, since it would likely mean that constructive administrative changes would be less likely to occur. Chapter three reviews conflicts that usually arise between the citizenry and the bureaucracy when public policy is being formulated and implemented. It then examines specific area of cooperation that could ease tensions between the people and the public service. The chapter also discusses some ethical theories and moral principles that are usually translated into codes of ethics for public employees in various countries. Finally, it argues how in industrialized countries and developing ones, the general knowledge and observance of administrative ethics could vastly reduce conflicts and increase cooperation between the bureaucracy and its clientele.

1

MICRO-BUREAUCRACIES AND DEVELOPMENT ADMINISTRATION

Most non-Western bureaucracies are composites of a series of informal micro-bureaucracies structured along political interests or modernizing approaches. These micro-bureaucracies flourish in the midst of rivalries, conflicts and tensions that are more often of a political rather than an administrative nature. Although they exist almost everywhere in the Third World, they are most readily observable in those countries that offer an optimum of conditions for their survival and operation.

This chapter considers the micro-bureaucracy phenomenon against the broad background of the non-Western world and will review some peculiar conditions in the Caribbean islands that show them to be an ideal laboratory for empirical research on micro-bureaucracies. Therefore, the often stated hypothesis that some distinctive features of the Caribbean bureaucracy could be integrated into some kind of loose "model" of Caribbean administration is being dismissed from the very beginning. However, the geographical area does offer a unique opportunity for testing theories about many varieties of non-Western administration already functioning in other non-industrialized countries.

After theoretically defining "micro-bureaucracy" and sub-categorizing it into two distinct groups, the chapter examines a series of tension-producing factors that affect the activities of each of the two groups. Most traditional Asian and African administrative systems are built upon — and survive by maintaining — a fluctuating network of rivalries, conflicts and tensions. These balanced tensions often serve as a stabilizing factor in these systems. In this chapter only those tensions that positively or negatively affect the strategy and work of the micro-bureaucracies are analyzed. In the final part, the role of micro-bureaucracies in development administration is pointed out and some suggestions are made as to how the theories advanced in this chapter could be best tested in the Caribbean political systems.

MICRO-BUREAUCRACIES

Micro-bureaucracies are small and informal organizations of bureaucrats that have the broad common aim of wishing changes that would benefit the entire social and political system. They are subdivided into two categories: those that are political and the non-political or administrative ones.

In this chapter small groups within the large bureaucracy which meet only for social reasons are not considered micro-bureaucracies. This is not to ignore the fact that most of these social groups spend a great deal of time discussing politics and that such political discussions often have important consequences in developing societies. As a matter of fact, most political micro-bureaucracies originate out of informal political discussions between members of the bureaucracy. Public employee unions, whose sole interest is to improve the welfare and working conditions of their members, will also be excluded from the micro-bureaucracy classification.

Political Micro-Bureaucracies

A political micro-bureaucracy is a group of bureaucrats who are interested in provoking a political change in the central government. It will tend to be a horizontal organization including bureaucrats from different ministries or departments who have a common educational or social background. The activities of a political micro-bureaucracy are often secretive, especially under a repressive government. Its technique of operation is similar to those of conspirators. It is more likely that the members of these groups will be in the higher strata of administration, including ministers, since they probably aspire to take over the government themselves in order to make the reforms they advocate. The members of these groups are referred to as policrats because they usually conceive of the government (or the management of the whole society) as run only by political experts, or in accordance with principles established by politicians.

Most dictators well know the way the political micro-bureaucracies operate and they must learn fast how to neutralize them. The late Emperor Hailé Selassié, who was a very enduring chief of state, has maintained control over the Ethiopian bureaucracy by playing the game of Shum-Shir ("up-down" in Amharic), a technique of alternatively raising and lowering his subordinates' status so as to maintain their loyalty without letting them become overly powerful. In the Caribbean, Fidel Castro's militia acts as an auxiliary bureaucracy to keep the formal bureaucracy loyal. The excessive zeal and loyalty of the militia is directed toward one man, the Chief.

The political micro-bureaucracies should not be confused with the situation existing in some non-Western bureaucracies that have become politically active because of lack of political orientation from their governments. These bureaucracies have assumed collective, growing political power in order to operate safely, as the French bureaucracy, a Western one, did during the third and fourth Republics when political instability was a permanent feature of the French government. Never in such instances did the bureaucrats seem to consider taking over the government.

From a purely administrative point of view, the activities of the political micro-bureaucracy are often negative. In its pursuit of its primary goals, it sometimes sabotages the administrative effort of other segments within the bureaucracy. A major tool used by policrats is the dissemination of rumors. These rumors are designed to achieve some of the following effects: a) reduce the prestige of the government by ridiculing its actions or misrepresenting its intention; b) unite different segments of the opposition into a broader organized action against the government; and c) ultimately provoke a change in the political system (Garcia-Zamor 1976: 70).

Administrative Micro-Bureaucracies

Administrative micro-bureaucracies have more open aims. They also want changes but only changes that strengthen the larger bureaucracy or increase its efficiency. Typically, the members of each of these groups are mostly concentrated in one ministry or department or in a few agencies performing in a related area. Because of the "team nature of their activities, they are primarily vertical organizations, with their members belonging to a variety of socio-economic groups. Since they are apolitical and their goals are not subversive, they can both recruit and operate openly. They are not altogether free of political pressures since they often advocate certain changes that might seem to be subversive. In many developing societies, constructive criticisms of the government or the bureaucracy are not tolerated to the extent they are in most modern industrialized societies. Thus, the administrative micro-bureaucracies may easily become targets of government retaliation. The members of these groups are referred to as "technocrats" because, contrary to the policrats, they want the government or the whole society to be run by technical experts, or in accordance with principles established by technicians.

In order to operate within a minimum margin of safety, it is extremely important for the administrative micro-bureaucracies to state clearly their aims to government representatives wherever they can be found so they will not be considered political micro-bureaucracies. This will not guarantee them government support of any sort since the chief bureaucratic planners of the regime will tend to belittle the reforms proposed by the administrative micro-bureaucracies in order to defend and justify their own strategies and techniques. However, cooperation can sometimes be achieved since the reforms that are being sought by the administrative micro-bureaucracies are limited to developmental goals or strategy and no change in the government is being advocated. The technocrats will join the efforts of the policrats for overthrowing the government only when they become convinced that the existing regime is either too corrupt or too incompetent to adopt the changes that they are promoting. In a non-military polity, when technocrats and policrats are allies, the government's chance of survival is extremely low. Most of the time, these alliances between technocrats and policrats are of short duration and the two groups usually revert to their antagonistic positions as soon as the government has been eliminated.

TENSIONS IN POLITICAL MICRO-BUREAUCRACIES

A series of factors contribute to the creation and maintenance of tensions within the political micro-bureaucracies. Some of them are briefly reviewed below.

Fear of Political Destruction

As the political micro-bureaucracies work toward change in government, leaders of the regime become increasingly aware of their activities and try by all means to stop them, because the primary concern of the government is its political survival. In the United States for example, the policies of an administration may come under virulent attack but no one will question the right of that administration to survive until the next election. In the non-Western world, with few exceptions, the government's right and ability to survive to the end of its term in office is in constant question. The president, or the prime or chief minister, is always building his political fences to "coup-proof" his government. That makes government very personal and tends to justify the assumption that developing countries need the spoils system.

Political Competition

Members of a political micro-bureaucracy are watchful of other groups with similar purposes that may undercut their efforts and beat them to the center of power. Because of the elitist nature of these groups, each will have a rather homogeneous behavior that reinforces their togetherness and contribute to exclude other kinds of people.

As elites in developing countries are socialized within the same class, their economic, social, and political attitudes tend to be similar. This very same factor might isolate them from the rest of the bureaucracy. The result of these presuppositions is a hypothetical tension that could as well be defined as "ecological isolation." The intense competition and rivalry tend to focus attention on political behavior within the bureaucracy rather than on a pragmatic approach to the function of administrating political decisions. The tensions thus arising are often external to the micro-bureaucracy rather than internal and could result in the inability of the micro-bureaucracy to efficiently carry out administrative enforcement of political decisions. To further complicate the situation, a hierarchical structure of authority and power would seem to be less defined and rigid within the political micro-bureaucracies where all bureaucrats tend to come from the same social and economic class.

Political competition is often directed solely toward participation in the decision-making process, but sometimes it is also promoted by a desire to be near people who are in power. In developing societies the fact that one is an intimate friend of a president assures him of great social prestige and of almost the same veneration as the government leader. A former president of a developing country once confided to the author of this book a very amusing anecdote. A few days after taking over, he had summoned to his office a good friend, who was at the time a bureaucrat and asked him what position he wanted in his government. ."..Secretary of State, Ambassador to the United Nations?" The friend refused all the positions offered to him. He wanted only a sinecure. He requested that he often be invited to palace parties where he would each time be allowed to say a few words in the President's ear in front of the other guests. Then the President was to smile and nod approvingly. For the bureaucrat that was enough. He knew that this open intimacy with the President would bring him prestige and all kinds of economic opportunities. This situation exists also in the United States and other developed societies. Membership in the intimate group of friends and informal advisers of President Bill Clinton, referred to as Friends of Bill (F.O.B.), for example, have ripped great benefits to several individuals.

The Large Size of the Bureaucracy

Although high administrative posts are limited, the lower bureaucratic echelons tend to be overstaffed. This situation is often caused by the absence of other employment outlets in the community. Small government jobs become sinecures that the government must dispense to ease unemployment. The mere size of the bureaucracy is a favorable factor for the political micro-bureaucracies because it allows them some anonymity. When the bureaucracy is very small, it is usually intimately linked with the political leadership, and each bureaucrat feels that he owes his job to the generosity of the palace. A disproportionately large bureaucracy would mean that many public servants at the lower levels will not be qualified or even formally educated; thus the bureaucracy would not be very responsive and would operate routinely. The poor performance of the bureaucracy then becomes one more reason for the political micro-bureaucracies to gain new support in their effort to provoke a change of leadership. The only danger is the increased probability that government spies are planted in the bureaucracy or that individual bureaucrats choose to report the activities of the political micro-bureaucracies in order to gain favors from the government of to become more secure in their positions.

The Presence of the Military

If the country has a military force it is probable that the activities of the political micro-bureaucracies will be paralyzed. This makes some of the Asian and African countries very poor prospects for their work. Most unconstitutional political changes in these countries are provoked by the military. In the same vein, the countries of the Caribbean Commonwealth are especially favorable ground for the operation of political micro-bureaucracies since these countries do not have military establishments. The small size of the Caribbean countries prevents the isolation of the military from the civilians, and both military men and civilians mingle to a great extent. In large countries, the military develops a corporate ideology and mentality, which is different from that of the civilian.

The presence of the military also represents a constant threat of sudden retaliation from the government. Without a military force, the political micro-bureaucracies can more easily neutralize government reaction if their activities and real motives are uncovered.

The term "military," as used in this section, does not apply to militia forces like the Cuban one. Castro's militia is, in a sense, a bureaucratic apparatus. Its members see their form of association with the regime as a political career. The formal Cuban bureaucracy has so little power and freedom that if political micro-bureaucracies had to operate in Cuba, they would have to do so within an extremely limited parabureaucratic structure.

One assumption here is that the bureaucracy of a developing nation is a political battlefield and that the triumph of one group of bureaucrats over the other determines if a policracy or a technocracy will run the government. The validity of this assumption with regard to countries in which there exists a strong military sector might be questioned. However, in such cases, the micro-bureaucracies are not located only in the bureaucracy. They extend to include prominent military leaders who sympathize with either the policrats or the technocrats.

TENSIONS IN ADMINISTRATIVE MICRO-BUREAUCRACIES

Instability of the Political System

The instability that characterizes the political systems of many developing countries is often a beneficial factor for the political micro-bureaucracies, but it usually leads to tensions in the administrative micro-bureaucracies. With the future of the political system in doubt, the technocrats would undoubtedly feel uncertain of their status. This bureaucratic insecurity could reasonably induce them to strive to strengthen the political institutions, thereby increasing political stability. However, this situation could also lead to a strong self-protective attitude, forcing them to abandon their modernizing ideals to support the status quo in an attempt to maintain their somewhat shaky positions.

A side effect of political instability might also be a brain drain of the best qualified members or potential members of the bureaucracy to foreign lands. Contrary to what is being claimed, there is no indication that at the present time there exits a massive brain drain problem in the Third World. Most of the public servants who resigned their positions in the seventies and the eighties in the low-income Commonwealth countries, for example, were "expatriates" and the vacancies were filled with returning natives who had studied abroad. In the case of two small Caribbean countries, Cuba and Haiti, there is some indication that these two governments have been hurt by the exodus of exiles. But in both countries, a new brand of specialist, of humbler social origin and educated in national universities, has slowly replaced the emigrated ones. Considering the selfishness of the pre-Castro Cuban bourgeoisie and the pre-Duvalier Haitian elite, it can hardly be argued that the two countries are more deprived now because of the missing oligarchs.

Disparity Between Bureaucratic Goals
or Ideals and Existing Conditions

The administrative micro-bureaucracy's aspirations for the state may be handicapped by the limited resources generally found in developing countries. Attempts at modernization and industrialization may be frustrated by these limitations, thereby incapacitating the administrative micro-bureaucracy working toward these goals. This explains in part why so many bureaucrats hold a variety of jobs outside their regular civil service appointments. Officials from the US Agency for International Development (USAID) and experts from the United Nations have suggested several remedies: higher pay, greater job security, more professional training and pride in the service. But if the principle of "cultural relativity" is applied here, these solutions suggested in accordance with the United States and other Western cultural standards do not conform to the cultural mood of some of the developing countries. It is not at all obvious that the efficiency of public administration would be increased by requesting a Latin American bureaucrat to spend his whole lifetime in one narrow bureaucratic job at a time. The desire to play several roles, to be engaged in different kinds of activity, to have contacts and friends in many different places is of much higher value in Latin societies. Thus it has been suggested that the elimination of this multiplicity would not necessarily improve the bureaucracy. Holding several jobs is often a psychological outlet for the bureaucrat to convince himself that he is actually doing something positive despite the adverse conditions. Another reason for bureaucrats to hold several jobs in developing countries is the lack of available qualified people. A positive factor here is that, under these circumstances, the technocrat's chance of rising to the top is greater than it would have been in a bureaucracy staffed with a great number of evenly qualified people. This probably leads to a better morale situation among the members of the administrative micro-bureaucracies.

Lack of Bureaucratic Expertise

The concept of expertise, as it is to be used here, involves a combination of formal specialized knowledge and extensive experience. Those lacking such specialized knowledge and possessing relatively limited experience would be considered devoid of bureaucratic expertise. As seen in the previous section, the limited amount of resources available to developing countries prevents them from hiring the best qualified people. When a new complex situation arises, such as a natural disaster, the limited experience of the officials may be inadequate for dealing with the situation efficiently and effectively. In developing countries, there is little tradition in the government for bringing in temporary outside expertise except for "foreign consultants" whose visits require planning with other governments or international agencies and other time-consuming arrangements. Thus the absence of a number of bureaucrats possessing bureaucratic expertise in different specialized areas would appear to be a tension-producing factor within any administrative micro-bureaucracy.

Usually in developing countries the bureaucracy is multi-functional. This multi-functionalism tends to cause overlapping of duties in the various structures, and not enough specific knowledge of the various problems and possible solutions. On the positive side, multi factionalism may promote the relative ease of rule formulation and enforcement. The distance from the administrative elite to the lowest bureaucratic official will not seem insurmountable. Communication from one level to the next is more easily accomplished than in a uni-functional bureaucracy. The individual bureaucrat has the opportunity to observe the effects of any administrative decision which he makes on those influenced by the decision. As a result, he is able to perform more effectively. Within the administrative micro-bureaucracy the high-ranking bureaucrat participates in the development of policy as well as in the administration of policy. For the members so involved, this reduces the frustration that has been developed without reference to the expertise of the bureaucracy, which means that the social and economic elites of the country will continue to be attracted to the bureaucracy.

Strict Adherence to Traditional Values

Strict adherence to traditional values within the bureaucracy may prevent the expression or acceptance of new ideas or the modification of existing modes of operation. In many developing countries where traditional emphasis is placed upon complete and unquestioning obedience to one's superiors, any attempt by a subordinate to suggest new ideas or more efficient ways of doing things would be discouraged or condemned. Adherence to such an authoritarian tradition within the bureaucratic structure would inhibit the creative potential of subordinates and permit the continuation of existing inefficiencies. A lack of formal education (as discussed in the following section) is sometimes responsible for the rigidity of some bureaucrats. They see no need for change, and are in fact quite suspicious of change or anything that could threaten their small, secure worlds.

Varying Degrees of Formal Education

Education is a process of becoming aware of the surrounding world. In a developing nation, it is a process of becoming aware of what is lacking in their world. In terms of formal education, it means the co-existence between the extremes of the well-educated and uneducated men and women. It would be difficult in a developed country's bureaucracy to find two bureaucrats with extremely different educational backgrounds working side-by-side in related tasks. However, this is a common feature in developing countries. Large segments of the bureaucracy are very often illiterate while a small group has received advanced training in some of the most sophisticated universities of Europe and the United States. Matters are complicated by the fact that the uneducated bureaucrat is blissfully unaware of his deficiencies. On a different level, tensions might arise between well-educated bureaucrats, especially if they have been trained in a variety of universities, including local and foreign ones. Although they will desire a stable pattern of development with the ultimate goal of political stability and some level of prosperity, they will often clash on matters of strategy for development, i.e., long-term vs. short-term goals. It will not be a conflict of interests, but rather a conflict about how changes should take place. To extend this example, it is obvious that short-term programs would be more popular with the majority of bureaucrats. However, some members of an administrative micro-bureaucracy might argue that while short-term goals and their attainment can prove to be a great morale booster, the completion of long-term projects are ultimately more beneficial. This clash of opinion could result in great bureaucratic tensions since one decision or another may cause the government to loose some of its popular support.

THE ROLE OF THE MICRO-BUREAUCRACIES IN DEVELOPMENT ADMINISTRATION

Although several definitions of development administration have been published, it is necessary to draw here an operational definition for the analysis that will follow. Development administration in this context is the bureaucratic process that facilitates or stimulates the achievement of socio-economic progress through the utilization of the talents and expertise of the bureaucrats. It involves the mobilization of bureaucratic skills for speeding up the develop-ment process. It should be assumed that, in developing countries, the primary task of the bureaucrat is to work toward the achievement of developmental goals. This is not true of Western countries that have already achieved a substantial level of development. In these countries, the major work for development is carried out by specialized public or private agencies, with the private sector (i.e. business) playing a vital role. In developing systems, development is synonymous with progress, and all the viable resources of the society are mobilized to achieve such progress. In this situation the bureaucracy becomes, first, the planner of the broad strategy that the politicians will propagandize, and later, the executor of the plans.

The role of the political micro-bureaucracies is a negative one in development administration. They are usually a group of policrats mainly interested in bringing about a change in government. Although many of them also wish progress, they tend to minimize their participation in the achievement of the government's officially-stated goals. Very often they will discredit good programs just to paralyze the government's effort. But most often they will just display complete apathy, thus leaving the door open for more outspoken enemies of the regime to attack from their own sectors.

The administrative micro-bureaucracies tend to play a positive role in development administration. They are the small groups of bureaucrats who prepare the government's plans. Although they may disagree with some of the specifics of the plans, they will usually share the government's ideals in terms of what should be done for the country's benefit. The members of the administrative micro-bureaucracies are essentially technocrats that execute the government programs.

RECOMMENDATIONS FOR RESEARCH

It could be safely assumed that in most developing societies, the percentage of policrats is much higher than of technocrats. This leads to the belief that the bureaucracies of the non-Western world are more politicized than those of the developed countries, a theory also advocated by various other writers. It should be uncontroversial then to state that in developing societies the number of political micro-bureaucracies operating in any single bureaucracy will exceed the number of administrative micro-bureaucracies. If one catalogs the different coup d'états that have occurred in recent years in the non-Western world and compares them with statistical data on progress achieved during that same period by the countries of that group, it will become quite clear that the aforementioned argument needs little additional empirical research to be sustained. However, other aspects of the theoretical framework of this chapter could be adequately tested in one or a group of countries of the Third World. The Caribbean countries, because of their size, their similarities, and other factors, would be an excellent area for such research. The broad features of these islands' polities have already been often pointed out:

a. They are geographically quite small;
b. They have only recently emerged from formal colonialism (the Hispaniola republics being the obvious exceptions);
c. They also have in many instances ethnically or racially mixed populations; and;
d. They are within the United States' "sphere of influence," from the geopolitical and economic point of view.

One might select in each of the Caribbean bureaucracies a certain number of public servants belonging to a variety of ministries within each bureaucracy and ask them a set of questions with a view to determining, first of all, if they should be considered policrats or technocrats. Their views of change should be explored and they would fall in one of the other category according to the kind of changes they envision as necessary, i.e. political or administrative. Additional questions would permit the categorization of those technocrats who are politicized and want also change in the main political structure. Through questioning on such matters as their views on developmental change, with whom they discuss politics and/or administration, etc., one would be able to determine if they are members of a political or administrative micro-bureaucracy. Eliciting the following information would help in the categorization: Do they associate with people of the same educational background? Do they discuss politics or administration primarily with bureaucrats in their agency or with other bureaucrats working at several other ministries?

Since most interviews of this nature might be difficult to conduct in some of the countries of the Caribbean (not to mention Cuba, where empirical research of this kind is plainly unrealizable), one could do some research about changes that have already occurred. Members of an active political micro-bureaucracy might be reluctant to reveal current information. However, if one asked a bureaucrat who is already in power (presuming that he is accessible to the researcher) about his associations before arriving at his present position, he might be more willing to speak. A native researcher could obtain the same information just by keeping a close watch on the bureaucracy, following local politics, and reading the daily papers. The native researcher will find ways of gathering the information and will be capable of preparing charts to illustrate the composition of both political and administrative micro-bureaucracies. Empirical field research could probably shed more light on the diverse ways the micro bureaucracies come into being.

If research were to be conducted in some of the larger developing countries, like Egypt and Brazil, one might arrive at some more definitive conclusions concerning the extent to which the theories advanced in this paper are applicable to all of the non-Western bureaucracies, independently of their size or culture. Such research in these areas would tremendously enrich the already existing, but unfortunately too confined, body of literature on informal politics and bureaucratic behavior in developing countries.

2

THE STRUGGLE OF SMALL
AND ISLAND STATES'
BUREAUCRACIES TO DEVELOP
TRADITIONAL ETHICAL VALUES

A PROFILE OF THE SMALL AND ISLAND STATES

It is difficult to arrive at a clear definition of "small state" and to decide how large an island can be before including it in a study of mini-countries. Each author seems to come up with his/her own arbitrary list considering a large variety of territorial sizes, including often both fully independent nations and dependent territories. Attempts at defining smallness are numerous and can be found in the emerging field of micro-states studies. Thirty years ago, a first definition was published by Benedict (1967), followed by works of the members of Working Group V of the International Association of Schools and Institutes of Administration. This group has been meeting yearly since 1983 to address issues pertaining to the administration of small and island states. Baker (1992) published a selection of their papers. One of these papers, by Raadschelders (1992) is a comparative study of definitions of smallness, and several others in the volume deal with the definitional problem.

The author has selected only states and islands less than 1,000 square miles that are independent nations or independent territories for inclusion in this chapter (Table 1). Only the Vatican City and the tiny Italian village of Seborga, with 356 inhabitants in about five square miles, which declared itself an independent principality in 1995, were excluded. Despite their autonomy, they lack other elements of a functioning political system. The sample in this chapter includes states as small as 0.75 square mile (Monaco) to one that measure 999 square miles (Luxembourg). Only four of the twenty-six states are not a member of the United Nations, and only two of them have literacy rate below 80 percent. An examination of Table 1 shows that most of them have some European cultural heritage and some type of viable economic mainstay.

However, twenty-five of the twenty-six countries are densely populated, Palau being the only one with a moderate population density (Table 2). The solution to the population problems of small states is a difficult one. The densely populated ones with non-European citizens find it very difficult to emigrate to larger industrialized countries. Furthermore, in these micro-countries, it is only a small minority of the people who are aware of the significance of rapid population growth, and often birth control campaigns antagonize both religious opinion and well-established patterns of behavior (Smith 1967: 22).

Even the most minuscule states have membership in one or more international organizations, Nauru being the only exception (Table 3). For many years, several small states did not want to apply for membership at the United Nations. The cost of maintaining a permanent mission in New York and paying their share of the Organization's annual budget were too high, as Maldive Islands confirmed by locating their small mission in the former Maldive Islands Stamp Shop in Manhattan (de Smith 1970: 10).

It is difficult to develop a profile of the small and island states. Except for their small territorial size, most of them seem to have very little in common. A classification of their economies by income and region (Table 4) place them almost evenly in every income group and subgroup and their geographical location span over four continents. Only the two small states situated in Africa, Comoros and Sao Tome and Principe, are in the low-income group. Singapore's world economic role is so disproportionate to her size that she is not even in the World Bank's classification. Despite her lack of manpower resources, Singapore remains a world market for several products, has a developed port with facilities for trans-shipping, processing and packaging operations which are essential to the region's economy (King 1973: 254). Singapore is presently making very swift progress in the field of robotics and other general technology indicators, such as semiconductor production. Her government has targeted electronics and computers as key industries for export-led growth (P. Kennedy 1994: 91).

The twenty-six small and island states considered in this paper are fairly integrated. Despite Neuman's findings (1976) about a lack of integration of small states, most of them are fairly homogeneous and share a common predominant culture, language, and history. Neuman's book covers also some very large segmented states, a fact that may explain her findings.

In a different analysis, a Human Development Index (HDI) developed by the United Nations Development Program (UNDP) (1995) places a majority of the small and island states in this paper among the highest in the world in human development (Table 5). The concept of human development was first introduced in 1990. For years, economists, politicians, and development planners have measured per-capita income to chart year-to-year progress within a country. As a result, a great deal of national development activity was focused on economic growth, often neglecting the human dimension of development. As a new way to measure human development, a team of leading scholars created a new Human Development Index (HDI) for UNDP. It revealed that even countries of a low per-capita GNP, like some of the small and island states, may rank higher on the HDI. The difference lies in the way national leaders set their priorities and allocate government funds and in the degree of freedom that citizens enjoy to act on their choices and influence their own lives.

The triple-component HDI considers life expectancy as one component not only for its own value but also because it speaks to health care delivery and the ability of people to live long enough to achieve goals. The second component, literacy, not only helps people to get and keep jobs but also assists them in understanding their surroundings and culture. The third one, purchasing power (per-capita income adjusted to account for national differences in exchange rates, tariffs, and tradable goods), demonstrates the relative ability to buy commodities and meet basic needs (Garcia-Zamor 1994: 113). For example, Malta, classified by the World Bank as an upper middle-class country, is ranked 34 in the HDI scale among 174 countries, ahead of several high-income countries. However, the HDI index can only reinforce the concept of formal status of a nation. As pointed out by Lagos (1963: 22), the real status of a country in the system of international stratification is based on three basic variables, economic stature, power, and prestige, all of them quite difficult to attain by the small and island states.

THE BUREAUCRACIES OF SMALL AND ISLAND STATES

Peters (1988: 3-4) views comparative administration as more than simply the accumulation of descriptive material about various different countries. He thinks that such description is sometimes useful as a means of beginning a more theoretical inquiry. The following discussion of some of the features of small and island states' bureaucracies will hopefully help understand their struggle to develop traditional ethical values. Furthermore, it might initiate a new area of research that will eventually enrich the growing literature on small and island states.

The majority of the small and island states, like many developing countries, are a composite world of two contrasting realities. There is on the one hand, the so-called urban elite, civil servants, politicians, military officers, and teachers, on the other, the rural poor who have very little participation in the planning or managing of development strategies that supposedly would help them. Often, the administrative framework of these countries have been set up by larger nations and/or international organizations primarily to handle the requirements imposed by the donors of foreign aid (Garcia-Zamor 1985).

In the previous chapter, the author introduced the concept of "micro-bureaucracy" in which a type of informal clique or faction of officials organized themselves to promote political or administrative objectives. The former category, which sometimes aims at the overthrow or transformation of an exiting regime, is composed of "policrats," whereas those drawn to the latter function are the "technocrats." In a book on three "small" island states in the Caribbean, he developed further that concept and made the point that the relative weakness or absence of a military force in most of the small island states means that groups of civil servants often carry out political functions, which elsewhere in the developing world, are performed by military officers. Another aspect of that work on small island states that is related to this chapter, is the formulation of a Typology of Creole Bureaucracies, derived from Aristotle and Robert Dahl's works, that included propositions about types and dynamics of transformation from one type of bureaucracy or political system to another (Garcia-Zamor 1977).

In small and island states, the management of development is usually concentrated in the public sector. Government economic development strategies are dependent on foreign aid. In Sao Tome and Principe for example, most competent civil servants work in some donors-financed projects. Their hard currency salaries make their wages 50 times higher than their previous national salaries. This imbalance makes it almost impossible for them to return to the civil service. They are constantly looking for positions in other donors-financed projects. In addition, those who are not involved in such projects spend considerable amount of time trying to get into one. This permanent race for positions outside the civil service takes place at every level, from chauffeurs, secretaries, to high ranking administrators, and make any attempt at administrative reform appear ludicrous (Garcia-Zamor 1998: 88-89). The author was the Non-Resident Chief Technical Advisor of a United Nations administrative reform project in Sao Tome and Principe in 1993. He experienced first hand how powerful foreign donors could not overcome the obstacles to reform that were coming from within the Santomean bureaucracy itself. Contrary to some notions, it is often more difficult to reform the bureaucracy on a small state than a large industrialized one. The total lack of other economic opportunities outside government employment makes it almost impossible to implement reform policies.

Differently from the larger and richer countries where public policy implementation involves countless routine tasks by the public servants, in small and islands states, like in most developing countries, the ultimate goal of public policy implementation is the attainment of developmental objectives expressed in the national development plans. These plans are usually inspired by foreign donors and are based primarily on expected technical assistance from abroad. In addition, many small and island states do not have the administrative framework to handle the requirements imposed by donors of foreign aid (Garcia-Zamor 1996: 198).

THE STRUGGLE OF THE BUREAUCRACIES
TO DEVELOP ADMINISTRATIVE ETHICS

The decades of the eighties and the nineties have witnessed considerable attention to the problem of administrative ethics in both industrialized and developing countries. Denhardt states that there is no clear consensus about what constitutes ethical administrative behavior and what that means for public administration. Should concern lie primarily with corruption, with the conflicting obligations of administrators, or with other dimensions of administrative activity (1988: vii)? For the purpose of this book, administrative ethics (i.e., accountability by public administrators or bureaucrats) and political ethics (i.e., accountability by the political leadership or the decision-making body) are discussed under the same umbrella as administrative ethics. The reason for this is that in the majority of small and island states, there really is no sharp demarcation between the two. Politicians not only make the decisions at the top, but at the same time act as administrators in carrying out governmental decisions to promote development.

There is an obvious difficulty in applying Western-developed ethical standards to administrative systems of different socio-economic and cultural environment. However, Frederickson suggests that the future ethics research agenda should "focus on the settings, professions, and cultures in which ethical issues occur and measure behavior against the cultural expectations and professional standards appropriate to the research context" (1993: 258). He further recommends that "once this is done, researchers should compare ethical standards and behavior between settings, professions, and cultures. In this way, the richness and variety of the common ethical themes and variations on those themes can be described" (1993: 259). Today, the term ethics has become such a popular one in every country or culture that a study of administrative ethics in small and island states is necessary and hopefully will open the door for future research in this direction. The main assumption in this chapter is that small and island states' bureaucracies find it difficult to develop traditional ethical values. In the following paragraphs there is a review of some ethical theories that are usually translated into codes of ethics for public employees in various countries. They clearly differentiate ethical behavior from unlawful ones and corruption.

Different ethicians have different theories that might be relevant in this case. But for the purposes of this chapter, only five prominent theories of ethics will be considered: a) egoism (the view that the standard that should be used to determine the best course of action is self-interest); b) conventional morality (the standard for determining right and wrong is the customary rules and practices of one's society); c) utilitarianism (that one should choose the course of action that produces the greatest benefit for the greatest number of people); d) duty ethics (the right action is the one that is done solely for the sake of duty); and e) virtue ethics (which places primary emphasis on forming good habits of character and acting accordingly) (Beabout and Wenneman 1994: 9-16).

There are several reasons why administrative ethics, based on these five theories will be a difficult thing to develop in the bureaucracies of the small and island states. One of them is the lack of awareness of ethical standards. Gortner suggests that the most important factors underlying the success of any bureaucrat attempting to behave ethically are his/her individual personality (or characteristics), his/her self-understanding, and the ability to apply that understanding to the ongoing organizational context (1991: 37). However, it is quite difficult to develop such understanding without the necessary awareness provided by a published code of ethics, on-the-job ethics training, and continuous open discussions of ethical issues. The author's own experience while teaching ethics to graduate students, mostly career civil servants, is that even United States bureaucrats often cannot perceive the difference between unethical and unlawful behavior.

Another reason why administrative ethics will be hard to develop in the bureaucracies of small and island states is the territorial size of these states. Administrative ethics is a concept that can better flourish in large-scale formal bureaucracies. Not only have these bureaucracies usually created an environment for the understanding and practice of ethical behavior (code of ethics, training etc.), but they are also tightly regulated by a myriad of public service laws and regulations. Their interpretation of administrative ethics has depended on two important features of the Western bureaucracies: their decentralized structure and their adherence to a set of characteristics patterned after Max Weber's bureaucratic model. Both of these features are often lacking in the bureaucracies of the small and island states. Even when they are formally present, in practice the bureaucrats ignore them.

Other factors that make it difficult for small and island states to apply administrative ethics are their geographical location, and tourism. Many small and island states are situated very close to larger developed countries (i.e., the Caribbean islands and the United States). They offer excellent opportunities for outsiders to attempt to corrupt their bureaucrats in order to be allowed to establish offshore bank accounts, smuggle drugs etc. Tourism is another negative factor. The saying is that small is beautiful. This is definitely so in the admiring eyes of Western tourists who want to experience a certain closeness to nature that their urban over-populated cities cannot provide. Unfortunately, anytime the number of pleasure-seeking tourists exceed, and sometimes double, the number of native residents, some negative consequences tend to follow.

All the five theories of ethics that were mentioned can help increase our understanding of the situation in small island states. Ethical egoism states that an action is right if it promotes self-interest. In the setting of small and island states, people tend to know each other and tend to value much more social contacts, even across socio-economic lines. The Weberian characteristics of a formal bureaucracy are hard to be accepted in such a context. Bureaucrats will not hesitate to bend the rules to help friends and relatives. They feel that it is in their best interest to act in a manner that will not marginalize them from the rest of society.

Conventional morality states that the standard for determining right and wrong is the customary rules and practices of one's society. Cultural heritage, national values, and the scale of a society play important roles in determining what might constitute a violation of administrative ethics. Possibly, a behavior that could be considered unethical in a large-scale society might be an acceptable one in a small-scale society. But here size alone in terms of territory and population does not determine the scale of a society. Benedict states that a large number of roles has to exist in the society. Quoting several other scholars, he makes the point that for a large scale society to exist, there must also be a condensation of society, multiplying social relations among more individuals, and a greater division of labor. Benedict admits that while this need not take place in a large population with a simple economy (as in the segmental societies), it is more difficult to occur in a very small-scale society (1967: 47). In this context, conventional morality might even vary among the small and island states. On the one hand, some of them are typical small-scale societies (Sao Tome and Principe, Comoros etc.), on the other, some can be considered large-scale societies despite their small territorial size (Singapore, Luxembourg etc.).

Utilitarianism states that one should choose the course of action that produces the greatest benefit for the greatest number of people. In small and island states, the bureaucracy and its clientele do have a shared interest, as distinct from their purely personal and private interests, and it is this common interest which holds them together and give them their identity. Discussing small groups within a larger society, Bond (1996: 211) observes that the existence of a common interest is important. It shows that there exists something that benefits all the members of the group. This is enough to kill purely egoistic individualism, for everyone is concern with the common interest of the group. Violating such principle can socially isolate individual bureaucrat, a situation hard to deal with in a small-scale society.

Duty ethics is the theory that states that a morally good action is one that is done solely for the sake of duty. The problem with duty ethics in small and island states is that family and social ties can be so tight that conflict may arise regarding which course of action is morally right. Sheeran states that duty is often defined as a moral obligation to do something or omit something. "There is a binding of the will to perform or not perform" (1993: 95). But D. F. Thompson distinguishes between two kinds of moral duties: those that are valid whether or not anyone is observing or acting on them and those that are not valid unless one has good reason to believe that others are also observing them (1987: 109). This can be quite a dilemma for an individual bureaucrat in a small and island state where often no civil service regulations and no codes of ethics firmly establish acceptable norms of conduct.

Since there is a large variety of political systems among the small and island states, each one of their bureaucracies might be facing a different political reality. Moore (1995: 32-33) states that under such situation public administrators sometimes find it necessary to challenge the wisdom of politically expressed policy mandates. They do so on the basis of their moral obligations to defend the public. However, there are times when public servants have to act on their own because either a weak or indifferent leader fails to oversee them. These can be dangerous times since bureaucrats can become abusive with impunity. A good example of that is what happened in Malta during the seventies and eighties when corruption flourished within the bureaucracy. Everything required a permit and there was almost a published tariff of bribes (Gaul 1993: 76).

Some ethicians claim that virtue is the most important element in the moral life. Virtue ethics places primary emphasis on forming good habits of character. Beabout and Wenneman (1994: 16-17) point out that this approach also has problems. The qualities of character that are considered virtuous and what is recognized as a virtue seem to vary from culture to culture. It is also unclear whether the same virtues apply to all people universally. So virtue ethics lacks universality in its application and suffers from a lack of clarity when applied to specific issues. One way to identify the presence of virtue ethics among bureaucrats of small and island states is to analyze their policy-making and implementation. Pops (1991: 265) mentions Rawls' focus on the role of government institutions in the fashioning of social justice. When bureaucrats contribute to fair economic and social policies, they exhibit virtue ethics and set the stage for and determine all other values.

THE FUTURE OF ADMINISTRATIVE ETHICS IN THE SMALL AND ISLAND STATES

The previous section of this paper established how difficult it is for bureaucrats of small and island states to be aware of and practice traditional administrative ethics. This is not surprising when one considers the many failures of public accountability in large scale societies. Caiden (1989: 26-28) discusses several shortcomings of their bureaucracies: the existence of incompetent political overseers, corrupt career public servants, an anti-democratic ethos, bureaucratic inertia and anonymity. Sembor and Leighninger (1996: 162) elaborate on the same theme. They state that the meaning of the word "public" in public administration seems to have splintered in the 1990s. Citing other scholars, they remark that the majority of the general American public does not believe that public administration is a particularly ethical or public-minded profession — almost everyone in public service is portrayed either as a power-hungry politician or a self-interested bureaucrat. At the same time, the voting public is widely characterized as apathetic, uncommitted, and uninterested in public affairs. But despite the apparent failures of applied ethics in the large-scale societies, a new awareness of the problem has contributed to more progress in the field.

Before discussing the future of administrative ethics in small and island states in this chapter, several attempts were made to diagnose their present ethical situation. Extensive bibliographical references were used to determine the level of ethical violations in these states. Since it was not possible to find the proper citations for all 26 countries, it was originally assumed that using fairly good and reliable library resources and the Internet, the results would be as scientific as any random polling sample. A major difficulty that soon arose with this methodology was that updated bibliographical references on the small and island states were scarce; thus the research relied only on the Internet. Using the World Wide Web search engine Alta Vista com advanced query, the number of general entries for each state was recorded. Then a count was made of the number of entries obtained using the three keywords: ethics, corruption, and accountability (Table 6). The result was that Singapore had the most entries in that category. However, because of the large number of general entries she had, only .05 percent of these were negative, not a far worse result than some of the other small and island states.

As pointed out earlier in the chapter, the scale of a society increases the more it is in contact with other societies. Thus a dramatic increase in communications with the rest of the world might foster the development of universalistic role-relationships and impersonal institutions now lacking in small-scale societies (Benedict 1967: 55). At the present time, big cities in North America and Europe are wired in the Internet for fast, heavy-data traffic, while the small and island states are not. But technology being presently developed might eliminate this imbalance in the early 2000s. A print journalist, E.Weise, reported in a Miami Herald article of March 17, 1997 that Telesedic Corporation, a company financed by two American billionaires, Bill Gates and Craig McCaw, plan to place 840 Volkswagen-size satellites about 435 miles above the earth to form a constellation that covers the globe. Since the cost of digging up Asia and Africa to lay millions of miles of wire would be absurd, using satellites, messages will simply bounce up into space and then come back down to receivers. When such a technology becomes fully operational, even the most isolated small and island states will start closing the general awareness gap that now exists between small-scale and large-scale societies. Reich (1992: 87) states that new technology already in place has created a "new web of enterprise" that will dramatically reduce that gap. People all over the world will be in direct contact with one another to continuously discover new opportunities. Administrative ethics will no longer be an alien concept for the bureaucrats of small and island states. Applied ethics will become an achievable objective for them.

TABLE 1
ISLANDS AND SMALL STATES
UNDER 1,000 SQUARE MILES

Country	Size Sq. Miles	Population	Cultural Heritage	Literacy Rate	Life Expectancy at Birth M/F	Economic Mainstay
Andora	181	72,766	French Spanish	100%	- / -	Tourism Sheep Tobacco
Antigua & Barbuda	171	65,647	British	90%	- / -	Manufacturing Tourism
Bahrain	268	590,042	Arabic British	85%	72 / 77	Oil Products Aluminum
Barbados	166	257,030	British	97%	72 / 77	Sugar Tourism
Comoros	719	569,237	French	57%	56 / 61	Perfume Textiles
Dominica	290	82,926	British	90%	75 / 80	Soap Tourism
Kiribati*	313	80,919	British	90%	- / -	Fishing Handicrafts
Liechtenstein	62	31,122	German French	100%	- / -	Machines Electronics
Luxembourg	999	415,870	German	100%	75 / 82	Steel Chemicals
Maldives	115	270,758	British	93%	65 / 68	Fish Tourism
Malta	122	375,596	British Italian	91%	76 / 81	Tourism Electronics
Marshall Islands	70	58,363	German Japanese	91%	62 / 66	Tourism
Mauritius	788	1,140,256	French British	83%	67 / 74	Tourism Textiles
Nauru*	8.2	10,273	German Australian	99%	- / -	Phosphates Mining

Country	Size Sq. Miles	Population	Cultural Heritage	Literacy Rate	Life Expectancy at Birth M/F	Economic Mainstay
Palau	188	16,952	American Polynesian	—	69 / 73	Tourism Fish
St. Kitts & Nevis	104	41,369	British	90%	- / -	Sugar Tourism
St. Lucia	238	157,862	British	80%	67 / 74	Clothing Tourism
St. Vincent & Grenadines	150	118,344	British	96%	71 / 75	Agriculture Tourism
San Marino	24	24,521	Italian	98%	- / -	Tourism Wool Goods
Sao Tome & Principe	386	144,128	Portugese	54%	- / -	Cocoa Coconut Products
Seychelles	176	77,575	French British	84%	67 / 74	Tourism Food Processing
Singapore	247	339,692	British	91%	75 / 81	Shipbuilding Oil Refining
Tonga*	290	106,466	British	93%	66 / 71	Tourism Fishing
Tuvalu*	9.4	10,416	British Polynesian	96%	62 / 65	Copra

* Not a member of the United Nations

Source: *World Almanac of Book of Facts*,1997

TABLE 2
DEMOGRAPHIC CLASSIFICATION

Country	Number of Persons per sq. mile	Country	Number of Persons per sq. mile
Andora	402.0	Micronesia	462.7
Antigua & Barbuda	383.9	Monaco	42,292.0
Bahrain	2,201.7	Nauru	1,252.8
Barbados	1,548.4	Palau*	90.2
Comoros	791.7	St. Kitts & Nevis	397.8
Dominica	285.9	St. Lucia	663.3
Kiribati*	258.5	St. Vincent & Grenadines	788.9
Liechtenstein	501.9	San Marino	1,021.7
Luxembourg	416.3	Sao Tome & Principe	373.4
Maldives	2,354.4	Seyhelles	440.8
Malta	3,078.5	Singapore	13,752.0
Marshall Islands	833.8	Tonga	367.1
Mauritius	1,447.0	Tuvallu	1,108.1

* Not a member of the United Nations

Note: All of the islands and small states can be considered densely populated (more than 250 persons per square mile). Only Palau has a moderate density (50 to 250 persons per square mile). None can be considered thinly populated (less than 50 persons per square mile).

Source: *World Almanac and Book of Facts,* 1997

TABLE 3
TYPES OF GOVERNMENT AND
INTERNATIONAL LINKS

Country	Type of Government	Head of State	Membership in International Organizations
Andorra	Parliamentary Co-principality	President of France & Bishop of Urgel	UN
Antigua & Barbuda	Constitutional Monarchy	Queen of England	UN, OAS, the Commonwealth
Bahrain	Traditional Monarchy	Emir	UN (WTO, IMF, FAO, World Bank, WHO), Arab League
Barbados	Parliamentary Democracy	Queen of England	UN (FAO, WTO, World Bank, ILO, IMF, WHO), OAS, the Commonwealth
Comoros	In Transition	President	UN (World Bank, FAO, IMF, WHO), OAU, Arab League
Dominica	Parliamentary Democracy	President	UN, OAS, the Commonwealth
Kiribati	Republic	President	The Commonwealth
Liechtenstein	Hereditary Constitutional Monarchy	Prince	UN (WTO), EFTA
Luxembourg	Constitutional Monarchy	Grand Duke	UN (WTO), OEDC, EU, NATO
Maldives	Republic	President	UN (WTO), WHO, IMG), the Commonwealth
Malta	Parliamentary Democracy	President	UN, (WTO, WHO, IMF), the Commonwealth
Marshall Islands	Republic	President	UN
Mauritius	Republic	President	UN and all its specialized agencies, OAU, the Commonwealth
Micronesia	Republic	President	UN
Monaco	Constitutional Monarchy	Prince	UN
Nauru	Republic	President	—

Country	Type of Government	Head of State	Membership in International Organizations
Palau*	Republic	President	UN
St. Kitts & Nevis	Constitutional Monarchy	Queen of England	UN (WTO), OAS, the Commonwealth
St. Lucia	Parliamentary Democracy	Queen of England	UN (IMF, WTO, ILO), OAS, the Commonwealth
St. Vincent & Grenadines	Constitutional Monarchy	Queen of England	UN (WTO), OAS, the Commonwealth
San Marino	Republic	Two Co-Regents appointed every 6 months	UN
Sao Tome & Principe	Republic	President	UN, OAU
Seychelles	Republic	President	UN, OAU, the Commonwealth
Singapore	Republic	President	UN (WTO, IMF, WHO), ASEAN, the Commonwealth
Tonga	Constitutional Monarchy	King	The Commonwealth
Tuvallu	Constitutional Monarchy	Queen of England	The Commonwealth

* Not a member of the United Nations

Source: *World Almanac and Book of Facts,* 1997

TABLE 4
CLASSIFICATION OF ECONOMICS
BY INCOME AND REGION, 1995

	Sub-Saharan Africa		East Asia & Pacific		Other		
Income Group	Eastern & Southern Africa	West Africa	East Asia & Pacific	South Asia	Europe	Middle East	Americas
Low Income	Comoros	Sao Tome & Principe					
Lower Middle Income			Kiribati, Marshall Islands, Microesia, Tonga	Maldives			St. Vincent, Grenadines
Upper Middle Income					Malta	Bahrain	Antigua & Barbuda, Barbados, St. Kitts & Nevis St. Lucia
High Income					Luxembourg, Andorra, San Marion		

Note: Only 19 of the 26 islands and small states were classified. Their economies were divided according to 1993 GNP per capita: low income, $695 or less; lower-middle income, $595-2,785; upper-middle income, $2,786-8,625; and high income, $8,626 or more.

Source: *World Development Report*, 1995

TABLE 5
HUMAN DEVELOPMENT INDEX (HDI) 1995

HDI Level	HDI Rank	Inslands and Small States
High Human Development	25	Barbados
	27	Luxembourg
	34	Malta
	35	Singapore
	37	St. kitts & Nevis
	44	Bahrain
	55	Antigua & Barbuda
	60	Mauritius
	62	Seychelles
Medium Human Development	69	Dominica
	79	St. Vincent & Grenadines
	84	St. Lucia
	118	Maldimves
Low Human Development	133	Comoros
	139	

Note: Only 15 of the 26 islands and small states were ranked. A composite index, the HDI contains three indicators: life expectancy; educational attainment; and real GDP (in purchasing power parity dollars).

Source: *Human Development Report*, 1999

TABLE 6
ENTRIES ON THE INTERNET

Country	Number of Entries on the Internet	Number of Entries with Keywords: Ethics, Corruption, Accountability
Andorra	12,657	0
Antigua & Barbuda	7,661	1
Bahrain	22,094	4
Barbados	23,094	2
Comoros	6,373	0
Dominica	11,648	2
Kiribati	6,465	1
Liechtenstein	15,723	3
Luxembourg	52,697	5
Maldives	8,906	1
Malta	33,946	19
Marshall Islands	6,627	4
Mauritius	15,606	6
Micronesia	10,032	0
Monaco	34,036	1
Nauru	6,464	1
Palau*	10,399	3
St. Kitts & Nevis	2,624	0
St. Lucia	4,727	0
St. Vincent & Grenadines	2,630	1
San Marino	13,971	1
Sao Tome & Princt	4,407	0
Seychelles	9,888	2
Singapore	185,949	90
Tonga	9,105	4
Tuvallu	5,612	0

Source: World Wide Web Search Enging Alta Vists.com Advanced Query

3

CONFLICTS BETWEEN THE BUREAUCRACY
AND ITS CLIENTELE:
A COMPARATIVE APPROACH TO
ADMINISTRATIVE ETHICS

This chapter will review the sources of conflicts between the bureaucracy and its clientele in both industrialized and non-industrialized societies, looking particularly at the situation in the United States, and in developing countries. This comparative approach allows for a greater understanding of the working of the bureaucracy in different environments. However, as Ferrel Heady stated: ."..any attempt to compare national administrative systems must acknowledge the fact that administration is only one aspect of the operation of the political system" (1996: 6). Therefore, the analysis in this chapter is done in a broader contextual framework that extends beyond the bureaucracy. The same theories of administrative ethics discussed in the previous chapter are reviewed and their contribution to a reduction of conflicts and to an increase in cooperation between the bureaucracies and their clienteles are discussed. It is often quite difficult for public servants to fully comprehend such an elusive concept as "administrative ethics." However, it is an important one in regulating the relationship between the bureaucracy and the citizenry. Finally, an administrative ethics prescription is offered as a possible remedy to the present situation.

SOURCES OF CONFLICTS

In Industrialized Countries

The newspapers of the industrialized societies are often full of stories about the battles between the government and the citizenry. These conflicts are partly the cause of the popular feeling against big government. Many citizens feel that the bureaucracy is too big and not efficient and responsive to their needs. As A. Downs explains, "...critics of 'big government' decry the gross inefficiencies of bureaus. In their opinion, bureau growth is a result of self-aggrandizement and represents a net loss to society" (1994: 39). However, when two American public administration scholars did some exploratory field study of a U.S. municipal government recently, the results revealed that citizens were accustomed to thinking of the cost of government but not its value or worth. After examining the relationship between citizens and government, the authors proposed a value-centered model that focuses on the worth of government to its citizens (Smith and Huntsman 1997: 309-310). This novel approach could alter the traditional negative views of citizens of the bureaucracy. The following is a discussion of some of the major areas of conflict between public bureaucracies and citizens.

The Level of Services Provided by the Government in Developed Countries: In developed countries, a large segment of the population is educated and is not afraid of getting into confrontational situations with the bureaucracy. Citizens in these countries like to feel that they are getting the maximum level of services. They think that it is the responsibility of the government to maximize their tax dollars and increase efficiency in the bureaucracy for a flawless delivery of goods and services to them. However, some factors such as race and income may affect the level of citizens' satisfaction when they visit government agencies. A study conducted in the 1980s in a large U.S. metropolitan area found that income had an effect on how people were treated by bureaucrats. Higher income individuals usually had higher expectations and a perception that they influenced the officials. Lower income individuals were more directly influenced by the officials and expected less from them (Hasenfeld 1985: 632). Robert Reich also discusses this situation in his book The Work of Nations. He wrote that the growing segregation of Americans by income, when coupled with the shift in the burden of financing public services from the federal government to the states and localities, has resulted in growing inequalities of service. Increasingly, where you live determines the quality of public service you receive (1992: 274).

Although the level and quality of services provided by the government in developing countries is extremely low, it is not usually a source of conflict. Citizens from these countries expect very little from their governments and they lack the initiative and resources to confront the bureaucracy if they are dissatisfied. In these countries, the bureaucracy is strongly associated with the ruling elites and responds quickly to their requests. But the general citizenry is not capable of openly confronting the bureaucracy.

Another factor that affects the existence or absence of conflicts in developed countries is the social and civic leadership that is found in specific sectors of the communities. A recent study found that awareness and social involvement are the most important variables in explaining citizen bureaucratic contacts (Serra 1995: 182). This means that the more awareness a citizen has about government, the greater the chance that he will contact an agency. Also, the more involved a person is in social groups, the greater the number of contacts will be. Since most communities have countless organized groups, people in developed countries tend to have many more direct contacts with the bureaucracy.

However, in the United States, local governments provide most services. Citizens generally have a better view of how their local government is running as opposed to State and Federal governments. Interestingly enough, some scholars have argued that although citizens feel negatively towards the bureaucracy, as a whole, they often had different views when questioned about the performance of the agencies with whom they have interacted (Lyons, Lowery and DeHoog 1992: 4). Charles Goodsell made also this point in a book in which he discussed the results of his surveys of citizen's attitudes toward agencies they have had some dealings with. He found out that bureaucrats were seen as:

> ...usually helpful, honest, responsive, adaptable, efficient, dependable, fair, friendly, respectful, considerate, [and] courteous. This is true on all levels of government and even in difficult, low reputation fields such as law enforcement, public welfare, and the Postal Service...(1994: 46)

In France, a 1997 poll revealed that 60 percent of those sampled responded favorably to the word "bureaucrat" despite the fact that 54 percent of French economic activity is the result of government spending, or that 25 percent of all workers work for the government. After quoting the poll's results and other statistics, George Will's June 23, 1997 Newsweek article, stated that "The French exemplify cognitive dissonance, a mild mental illness common to, indeed pandemic in, democracies. It consists of embracing starkly incompatible ideas and desires."

The Weberian Structure of the Western Bureaucracies: Another reason why conflicts arise between the bureaucrats and citizens in the developed countries is the very structure of the bureaucracies. Many citizens feel that bureaucracies are so complex and hierarchical that they are removed from the individual needs of the population. They also think that in order to get something done they have to go through too many rules and procedures, although as mentioned earlier, their attitudes tend to change after they have dealt directly with a government agency. Therefore, the complex nature of the bureaucracies is in itself a cause for potential conflicts.

Successful policy implementation in developed countries has depended on two important features of the Western bureaucracies: their decentralized structure and their adherence to a set of characteristics patterned after Max Weber's bureaucratic model. This may appear to be a sweeping generalization since there is not sufficient similarity among so-called developed societies with regard to adherence to Weberian bureaucratic norms. Certainly there are very different structural patterns of policy implementation in unitary versus federal systems (Garcia-Zamor 1996: 197 and 207). But in general, the main characteristics of the Weber's model tend to alienate the bureaucracy from its clientele. The model regulates rigidly the official duties of the bureaucrats, limits their sphere of competence, submits them to strict and systematic discipline and control in the conduct of their offices, presents them with a consistent system of abstract rules, and establishes a rigid hierarchical structure and a constant supervision by someone with authority. The fact that the model also prescribes that the bureaucrats should be chosen on the basis of technical qualifications and become integrated in a career does not reduce the aloofness of its formal framework. Therefore, some citizens feel that their individual problems cannot be addressed properly because of the structure of the bureaucracy.

The Perceived Controversial Nature of a Given Policy: Some of the conflicts between citizens and bureaucrats in developed countries originate from the perceived controversial nature of a given policy, program objective or legislation that is not in step with the accepted values of a certain segment of the society. Fortunately, in the United States, the judicial branch of the government can mediate the conflicts in an authoritative and final manner. Laws regulating gun control, welfare programs, gay rights and abortions have been particularly controversial.

Another area that creates conflicts between citizens and the bureaucracy in the United States is foreign aid policy. Things such as military interventions in the Middle East, Somalia, Haiti, and other places cause some Americans to wonder why the United States has to be the world's policeman. Also, monetary assistance to foreign governments and favorable international trade accords for some countries disturb some Americans who think that such money could be better used domestically to help the poor and protect small businesses.

The Vast Ethnic, Racial, and Religious Diversity of the Industrialized Societies: There are very few developed countries that are not facing a problem with immigration. The search for jobs and a better life has attracted large number of immigrants — both legal and illegal — to these countries. Another cause for conflict is the ethnic, racial and religious diversity created by these immigrants. In the United States, Affirmative Action and Minority Preferences laws have incited great conflicts between some citizens and the bureaucracy. These laws were designed to correct past practices of racial and gender discrimination. Their objective was to give extra assistance to minorities and women to achieve a balance among public employees with regards to the demographics of the general population. To most Americans, this seemed to be a well founded solution to remedy past injustices. But to some people, Affirmative Action is blatantly discriminatory because it asserts that one segment of the population should receive preferential treatment over the rest of the population.

In Developing Countries

Developing countries face many challenges. Many of these challenges lead to direct conflicts between the citizens and the bureaucracy, and often between the international community, the government and the citizens. The following are some of the factors responsible for these conflicts:

Structural Adjustment Program: Structural adjustment is one of the main sources of conflict between the citizens and the bureaucracy. The term has received different definitions by diverse scholars. For example, a recently edited volume with twelve essays provides several different definitions for structural adjustment (Schydlowsky 1995). However, the essential idea behind it is that if African countries or developing countries successfully reformed their economies in a neoorthodox way with the help and direction of the International Monetary Fund and The World Bank, then new international private bank lending and direct foreign investment would be available (Harbeson and Rothchild 1995: 50). These neoorthodox reforms are designed to jump start an economy for entry into the world capitalist system. Countries are given deadlines by which they must begin to reduce the size of their bureaucracies, privatize government-owned enterprises, end government subsidies of popular consumption items and devaluate artificially inflated currency.

The structural adjustment programs strongly encouraged by the International Monetary Fund and supported by the World Bank have proven politically and socially disastrous for many Third World countries (Garcia-Zamor 1994: 112). Africa, in particular, has long felt isolated from the world economy, was kept in the position of being a source of raw materials, and forced to import manufactured goods. Accepting the comprehensive reforms insisted upon by The World Bank and the International Monetary Fund reminded the Africans of past colonial policies. These reforms do not take into account the precarious political situation of some of the governments. Often, the structural adjustment policies have caused anti-government protests and riots and have been responsible for the overthrow of previously popular leaders. However, some authors note that to blame all the increase in poverty on the adjustment process is unfair. It would be as reasonable to blame it on the unwise policies and excessive borrowing that made the adjustment necessary (Morley 1995: 191).

Human Rights Violations: Another source of conflict is the often dismal human rights record of some of the developing countries. Many international organizations argue for the universality of human rights. This idea states essentially that all people are endowed with certain rights simply by being human and that it cannot be left up to a government to legislate which of those rights will apply in a particular territory. The idea is backed up by the Universal Declaration of Human Rights, passed unanimously by the United Nations in 1948 (Amnesty International 1993: 103). A recent illustration of this situation came to light in 1997 when Amnesty International and Kenyan rights groups said that Kenya needed extensive legal reform to ensure free and fair elections, and international observers to document human rights abuses. An estimated 1,500 people were killed and 300,00 were forced to flee their homes in the 1991-95 state-sponsored violence in the Rift Valley and Nyanza provinces (Ibid). Opposition parties, clergy and human rights activists in Kenya have long demanded the repeal of repressive laws that were introduced by the British colonial administration to clamp down on independence movements and that remain on the books. The laws permit officials to detain people without trial, restrict their movement, censor media and license public rallies.

Many of the developing countries are ruled by dictators who use their parabureaucratic armed forces to crush any opposition perceived as threatening. Free press is usually non-existent and the bureaucrats, anxious to keep their positions in an environment with no other job prospects, tend to be servile. The population fears them. Organizations like Amnesty International have continuously exposed these human rights violations to the world. In a publication on such abuses in the 1990s, it describes how government agents killed people for their political views, for belonging to a particular community, or simply for being poor. Every day, people seized by government agents vanished into secret custody as if they never existed. They simply "disappeared" (Amnesty International 1993: 1).

When the international community brings these charges to the attention of the government in question, the response is frequently two-fold. The charges are often vehemently denied and the foreign human rights organizations are sharply criticized for their negative reports. If they are not denied, then the human rights violations are often justified in the name of national security.

Both of these issues, economic liberalization as described above in the section on structural adjustment program, and the protection of human rights, represent very complex areas of conflict. They are made extremely difficult because they involve three entities: the international community, the government in question, and the citizens of that particular nation. In every case, the alliances differ, making it necessary to address conflict on a case by case basis. With such slow and meticulous work required, it appears as though these conflicts will not disappear very soon.

The Adoption of the Weberian Structure: As in the case of the industrialized countries, but for very different reasons, the structure of the bureaucracy is a source of conflict in developing countries. Many of these countries have adopted Max Weber's bureaucratic model for a variety of motives. Some feel that it represents a channel to economic development, since it is so successful in the West. Others have simply accepted it when imposed by foreign technical teams applying programs of administrative reforms (Garcia-Zamor 1997: 79-100). However, many of the characteristics of the Weberian model, reviewed earlier in this chapter, are inapplicable to developing countries. "Specialization," "institutionalized procedures," "impersonality," "orientation toward the office rather than the person," "universalism," "continuity of policy assured by files," and "separation of the incumbent from ownership of the means of production" cannot really work in societies that lack economic infrastructure, communication, training and/or education, among other things. In addition, in the smaller countries, everybody knows everybody else and it is part of one's social role to "help" friends and relatives. A prominent Indian scholar describes this phenomenon eloquently while discussing the paradoxes of his country's bureaucracy:

> Extreme impersonality combined with ready susceptibility to personal pressures and interventions. Public servants may be theoretically preoccupied with correctness and propriety, but in practice they may go along with endless irregularities and improprieties. Similarly, the pursuit of absolute justice and uniformity in civil service rules, regulations and

procedures often lead to glaring anomalies and injustices. It is a curious reflection on attitudes and thinking that Indian public services are willing to tolerate such contradictions between theory and practice (Jain 1989: 124).

Citing a report of the U.K. Overseas Development Administration that summarizes a continuous deterioration of the public sectors in most of Africa in the eighties and the nineties, Elliot Berg (1993: 199) blames this situation partly on the breakdown of basic management systems and partly on the inadequacies in salary and structure. The lack of adequate salary discourages the bureaucrats from delivering services efficiently. Worse, in some cases, it motivates them to solicit bribes before complying with routine requests from citizens. This can be a source of tensions and conflicts.

An examplary source of diminishing efficiency in the bureaucracy of a developing country caused by low salaries and overstaffing is the case of the Republic of Mali. The government of Mali's expenditures for personnel in the early 1990s were absorbing such a great portion of the national budget that very reduced funds were left for other basic expenditures, such as the buying of office supplies to allow the ever increasing bureaucracy to do its work. The lack of equipment and materials became one of the major reasons for the low productivity of the Malian civil service. In several cases, the number of secretaries was much greater than the number of typewriters available and the number of government chauffeurs greatly exceeded the number of functioning vehicles. Expenses for equipment and materials had never gone higher than 5 percent of the national budget since the late seventies, while 79 percent of the allocations went to expenditures for personnel (Garcia-Zamor 1992: 139).

A Lack of Citizens' Participation: While much conflict exists between citizens and public bureaucracies in both industrialized and developing countries, there is a growing feeling of cooperation between the bureaucracies and the citizens in the more advanced countries. This is attributable in part to a growing number of citizens who are getting involved in public issues there to try to find solutions for today's complex problems. In many industrialized countries, the public servants reduce conflicts with their clientele and create cooperation by simply finding out where the public interest lies. They do so through organized groups and the media. They also try to involve the citizens in policy making boards and community councils to foster a feeling of cooperation. This allows them to make effective policies that meet the needs of the citizens. Such an approach, absent in developing countries where participation is rare, minimizes the existence of conflicts between the two groups.

Most of the developing countries are a composite world of two contrasting realities. There is on the one hand, the so-called urban elite, bureaucrats, politicians, military officers, and teachers, and on the other, the rural and urban poor who have no participation whatsoever in the making and implementation of public policies that supposedly would help them. Furthermore, in developing countries, the bulk of the population does not understand the process of public administration and economic development. Although, at the local level, people may be in a better situation to perceive the needs of their community or region than the bureaucrat who is operating in the capital city, the latter's global objective encompasses many variables that are not manageable at the local level. A decentralization of the bureaucracy is badly needed in most developing countries.

In these developing countries, most bureaucrats see themselves and are seen by the citizens as instruments of regulation and control. An African scholar writes that in Africa, the dominant view of administrative ethics has tended to be "law and order" oriented. He asserts that virtually all African countries are still more preoccupied with political questions than with those of administration (Moyo 1994: 527 and 537). This is also true in many of the other developing countries. It is not surprising that in such contexts, any attempt at increasing citizens' participation in the public policy process would involve changes that may affect strong vested interests. However, continuous pressures from outside donors and lenders have led many developing countries, even those with authoritarian regimes, to accept incremental changes to establish and increase citizens' participation.

The following are some of the reasons why real public participation will be difficult to achieve in developing countries:

- A centralized political system which views local initiatives with some suspicions;
- Scarce resources and the important role played by political priorities;
- The national bureaucracy tends to rule out participatory methods as an obstacle to the economies of scale that are sought;
- Lack of coordination at the national level where the bureaucracy is not presently capable of formulating coherent policy strategies.

THE ADMINISTRATIVE ETHICS PRESCRIPTION

The enforcement of ethical conduct is a growing problem in both developed and developing countries. Several governments, especially in the industrialized societies, have set up mechanisms to cope with problems such as conflict of interest, the taking of bribes, nepotism, and other obvious violations of accepted rule of decent conduct. Although the question of how administrative ethics could reduce conflict between the bureaucrats and the citizens has not been addressed before in the literature, it is an important one to explore here since it goes to the core of such concepts as "good administration" and "good government." Denhardt states that "ethics is concerned with the process by which we clarify what is right and wrong and by which we act on what we take to be right; ethics involves the use of reason in determining a proper course of action. Ethics is the search for moral standards" (1995: 108). Two other authors relate the application of ethics even more to the delivery of services by the bureaucracy. They write that the most basic, fundamental moral principle is the principle of respect and suggest that one easy criterion that can be used by an individual (in this case a bureaucrat) to determine if he is treating someone (a citizen) with respect is to consider whether his action is reversible. In other words, would he want someone to do the same thing to him that he is about to do to that person. This is the basic idea involved in the Golden Rule: "Do unto others as you would have them do unto you" (Beabout and Wenneman 1994: 50). If public servants treat the citizenry with respect, it is obvious that conflicts between the two will be greatly reduced.

Administrative ethics is usually shaped principally by the politics of the place but it is also a reflection of the culture of the people. A Chinese scholar writing about Hong Kong stated that administrative ethics there represents a curious mix of modern Weberian notions on the one hand and traditional Confucian values on the other. He asserted that:

> Insofar as culture represents a system of shared values, perceptions, attitudes and beliefs which characterize a community, a study of culture is definitely relevant to our exploration of the administrative arrangements and their attendant ethical implications for Hong Kong as a Chinese society (Lui 1994: 488 and 491).

In 1996 and 1997, the City of Miami in the United States, was shaken by some notorious cases of corruption: several judges, the City manager, one of the City commissioners, the director of the Port Authority and several other public servants were indicted. This flurry of cases made some people wonder if the City was not a crossroads for corruption and how much its multi-lingual, multi-ethnic, and multi-cultural characteristics might be responsible for this situation. In a way, Miami is a good example of what Fred Riggs characterized as a "prismatic society" in one of his best known books (1964), a place where shades of development and under-development intertwine to reveal a unique culture that could be associated at times with the industrialized Western societies, and at other times with the Third World. One of the most fundamental, and elusive, question that arose in the Miami case was: "What makes people who aspire to do good get involved in something so bad, often for so little?" Tom Fiedler, a political editor at The Miami Herald in a June 8, 1997 article, interviewed several experts. A brief summary of their statements reveals how ethical violations take root in the behavior of previously impeccable bureaucrats:

- it is rare that an honest person wakes up one day and decides to go crooked;
- there are a lots of steps between doing things that are legal, but not totally ethical, until you do something that is illegal;
- the topsoil [of honesty] begins to erode and comes lower and lower until the step into corruption isn't so high;
- corruption is usually the end result of innumerable, incremental favors offered and accepted;
- there is the atmosphere that being a public official entitles you to special favors;
- eventually, a mindset takes hold that exchanging favors is the norm;
- a new Rolex and some cash can be rationalized as an entitlement for years of hard work (Fiedler 1997).

Beabout and Wenneman make the same point from a different perspective. They state that prudence is practical wisdom... the ability to apply moral principles to specific cases:

People are not born with this ability. It is developed through experience in making moral decisions. Just as athletic ability can be improved through physical training, and musical skill can be augmented through repetition, prudence is a habit that can be developed with practice. Good decisions pave the way for more good decisions (1994: 74).

It is clear that the administrative ethics prescription that might work in industrialized Western societies might need to be modified to fit developing countries. Even among countries of the same level of development but with different political system, some adjustments are needed for the prescription to be effective. In the United States for example, the prosecutory-judicial method is plainly needed but experience there as elsewhere seems to suggest that it needs to be supplemented by other measures. In November 1994, the first International Conference on Ethics in Government took place in Washington,

D.C. and more than one hundred delegates, the majority of them from developing countries, initiated a dialogue. Such a gathering clearly demonstrated that the worldwide expansion of ethics programs has generated an international ethics community. Part of the debate was on common and shared values: ethical values which cross cultures (Bigelow 1995: 5-9

The administrative ethics prescription suggested in this paper is taking into account the myriad of cultural and political differences between countries to suggest a simple, universal approach to reduce conflicts between bureaucrats and citizens. It contains five elements: a) establishing a system of bureaucratic accountability; b) monitoring on-the-job behavior; c) keeping a watchful eye on conspicuous displays of wealth; d) preparing and publicizing codes of ethics; and e) teaching ethics and values.

Establishing a System of Bureaucratic Accountability: Although excessive control can disrupt administration and create red tape, it is unrealistic to apply the concept of "voluntary compliance" in many countries. A control system with sanctions is necessary. Each country will need to establish its own indigenous system that will fit not only with its political reality but also with the culture of its society. But the basic principles of honesty should not be sacrificed with weak rationalizations such as the extremely low income of public servants in most developing countries.

Three American scholars observed that in the United States system an excess of control might discourage some able people from entering public service while a neglect of gross abuse might in time undermine people's confidence in free government (Dimock, Dimock and Fox 1983: 100). But two other American public administration scholars stated that in the United States, and possibly many developed countries, the real-world situation leaves administrators responsible for resolving uncertainties that remain when a control system is in place. Their use of their discretion depends heavily on their internal compasses — a matter of character, devotion to the public service, and respect for the faithful execution of the law (Fesler and Kettl 1996: 379).

This point is well taken and proves that the mere existence of elaborate systems of control is not sufficient. Many examples can be found in the growing literature on public administration in developing countries written by public administration scholars from these countries. Dale Olowu and Victor Ayeni reviewed numerous accountability mechanisms that exist in the Nigerian public service focusing on some specific accountability instruments and their modes of operation and found that public accountability still can be strengthened in Nigeria (1989: 137-152). Gaspar K. Munishi explored public service accountability in relation to the management of the Tanzanian economy and showed how the lack of accountability frustrates the very process of development management in the various institutions of the Tanzanian state (1989: 153-167). Finally, a fourth native African academician, Godfrey G. Muyoba, discussing public accountability in the Zambian public service, wrote that there is ample evidence to show that financial control mechanisms which exist within ministries and departments are generally ineffective (1989: 174-176). In all these African countries, a system of bureaucratic accountability exists. But it has not been enough to ensure the faithful application of ethical standards by the bureaucrats.

Monitoring On-the-Job Behavior: Administrative ethics is not only the abstention from corrupt and unlawful behavior, but also the constant application of moral principles to job performance. However, the moral knowledge of bureaucrats is often quite limited since such knowledge involves a familiarity with abstract principles. Moral knowledge can be so abstract that it becomes difficult for the bureaucrat to see how it applies to particular cases. Beabout and Wenneman suggest that in applying theoretical principles to the facts and circumstances of a particular case, the bureaucrat should think in terms of "middle level moral principles":

> These are moral guidelines that are at an intermediate level of abstraction. They are not so removed from the concrete particulars that it is difficult to see how they apply. On the other hand, they are abstract enough that they apply to a relatively broad range of factual circumstances (1994: 73).

These middle level moral principles are actually the various codes of ethics that exist to guide the behavior of civil servants, members of professional organizations, and others. It is quite important that the public service of both developed and developing countries adopt such Codes of Ethics and publicize them throughout the government. This will contribute to the creation of a work environment where administrative ethics will be applied. Of course, as in the case of the system of bureaucratic accountability, the mere existence of a Code of Ethics is not enough to prevent corruption and ill-treatment of the citizenry. The elements of control discussed above in the section on establishing a system of bureaucratic accountability should be reinforced by a system of distribution of awards and sanctions.

In addition to a Code of Ethics, ethics legislation should be enacted to deal with the following:

- *Gifts and honoraria*. The question is whether to allow any, and if so, which ones. Many developed societies have put strict limits to the monetary value of gifts that can be accepted by elected officials and bureaucrats. Although loopholes still exist in most places, the possibility of being caught and prosecuted limit their use;

- *Post-employment*. This is a practice that allow a retiring bureaucrat to "sell" his knowledge of inside information to a former client in order to try to influence his former work environment in the making of decisions affecting his new employer. Even in developing countries, a time limit should be legislated to regulate such "revolving door" practice;

- *Nepotism*. Although most developed societies have already legislated rules against nepotism, such legislation is still rare in most developing countries. This is where it is the most needed because these countries have a weak economy, an absence of strong private employment sector, and cultural mores that put loyalty to family and friends first. These factors explain why their over-staffed bureaucracies are usually the major, if not the only, employer.

Many other areas, such as outside employment (an accepted practice in developing countries where bureaucrats are poorly paid) and no-bid contracts (to favor friends, relatives and donors), need also to be regulated.

Keeping a Watchful Eye on Conspicuous Displays of Wealth: It is difficult to understand why a conspicuous display of sudden wealth (like a bureaucrat buying a luxury car worth three times his annual salary) does not click ethical investigations in many countries. Again, cultural differences, not the level of development, might play a role there. A good example of that is the case of the City of Miami that was discussed earlier in this chapter. Although being a large cosmopolitan city in the largest industrial society of the world, the ethical scandals that plagued Miami could have been detected much earlier if the lifestyle of some of the violators was carefully monitored. Fiedler, in a Miami Herald article of June 8, 1997, stated that in more hide-bound communities of the United States (such as Omaha or Des Moines), someone flaunting riches is likely to encounter questions from the locals about where that money comes from. But not in Miami, he quoted an expert as saying: "The question in Miami will probably be, 'How can I get a piece of that money?'." (Fiedler 1997) This is a situation that is not dissimilar to what might happen in many of the developing countries.

Harriet McCullough states that financial disclosure is the cornerstone of any law intended to prevent abuse of public office for personal financial gain (1994: 252). She writes that:

> Ethics legislation may focus on public disclosure of personal financial information and the receipt of gifts and favors by public officials from those with whom they are doing business. This is a 'let the buyer beware' approach based on the premise that public officials or employees will conduct themselves appropriately out of concern about public scrutiny (246).

Although such financial disclosure laws exist in several developed countries, there are quite rare in developing countries. When they do exist, they are not strongly enforced.

Teaching Ethics and Values: The National Association of Schools of Public Affairs and Administration (NASPAA), the accrediting agency of public administration programs at the master level in American universities, has been urging its member-institutions for many years to include the teaching of ethics in their curricula. A recent article published in the official journal of the American Society for Public Administration, Public Administration Review, investigates what differences ethics education make in the life and behavior of men and women in pursuit of public service careers. The author identified a small number of schools that require Masters in Public Administration (MPA) students to complete an ethics course, and have had this requirement in place for at least five years. MPA alumni from these schools were surveyed. Most of them stated that ethics education was having a positive influence on them. The data collected also suggests that the ethical environment of the educational program must be taken into account in order to obtain a greater understanding of ethics education outcomes (Menzel 1997: 224).

The public bureaucracies of both the developed and developing countries need continuous training on ethics as part of their educational and professional enhancement for employees. This training should be mandatory to all public servants. The knowledge of principles that will guide them in dealing with their clienteles and the practice of ethical decision-making will not only reduce conflicts but will improve the overall image of the bureaucracy. The governments of both the developed and the developing countries need to establish guidelines to educate the public, the candidates for elective office, elected and appointed officials and other public servants as to the required standards of ethical conducts, and also need to enforce those standards of conduct. One of the problems in this area is that the places where an ethics education is the most needed are usually the more resistant to teach ethics.

A SUMMING-UP

Basically, the bottom line is that there is always going to be conflicts between public servants and the public, especially in the United States, which has a culture of conflict. Properly controlled, these could be healthy. The manner in which these conflicts are handled will determine if their outcomes will be positive or not. Positive outcomes might be achieved more often if the citizens are treated with respect and dignity. In developing countries, public servants have always been seen as the allies of the elites and most of their services are delivered to these elites. Unfortunately, this odd and inequitable phenomenon is growing in many industrialized countries, as described in an earlier section of this paper.

Ethical behavior must begin at the highest level and be reflected in the laws affecting the citizenry, then it can move down through the application of these laws by the bureaucrats, so that when citizens come in contact with public employees, they feel that they are being treated fairly. The increased knowledge and practice of ethical standards at all levels of government will reduce conflicts between the bureaucracy and its clientele. This in turn will improve the public's attitude towards government and its bureaucracies.

Despite the hierarchical nature of the bureaucracy, part of the moral decision-making process consists of "taking a stand" on issues that perhaps are not fully accepted by everyone in the bureaucracy. Taking a stand and making moral decisions facilitate the delivery of services to citizens. Two American scholars tackle this concept thoroughly by explaining that public officials underestimate the importance of taking stands: "Virtue for public officials in a democracy lies in great measure in taking stands in a way that elevates and dignifies public enterprises, in a way that makes them more consistent with what would be determined to be in the public interest..." (Moore and Sparrow 1990: 160).

As a public servant, it is not enough to adhere to rules and regulations. It is the moral responsibility of bureaucrats to take actions that would not violate any of the ethical theories and moral principles, hence making their decisions morally acceptable. When acting morally, public officials become more effective and efficient. This enhances not only productivity and equity, but it allows for citizen cooperation and satisfaction and reduces conflicts between the public service and the citizenry.

PART II

ETHICS AND DEVELOPMENT IN THE NON-WESTERN WORLD

The two chapters of Part II discuss the conflict between Western and non-Western standards in the bureaucracies and organizations of developing nations. In most industrialized countries, the hiring process is the first step in structuring an ethic work force. The Weberian principles have been instrumental in helping them do so. But problems arise when these principles are adopted in cultures where the public servants are not ethically committed. In some of these cultures there is a tendency to believe that the Weberian model of bureaucracy is necessary for a society to develop. However, many of the characteristics of the model are often inapplicable to small and developing societies.

In developing countries, the management of development is usually concentrated in the public sector. Governmental economic development strategies place great power in the centralized national bureaucracies, which are sometimes heavily dominated by incompetent and/or corrupt officials. In other cases, the inadequacy of the central government administrative structures complicates the tasks of project management. Chapter four highlights the various administrative and political risks involved when bilateral and/or multilateral donors try to circumvent the many obstacles created by state intervention and suggests new approaches to development project management to minimize the conflicts between donor organizations and recipient country organizations.

Successful policy implementation in developing societies has depended on two important features of the Western bureaucracies: their decentralized structure and their adherence to a set of characteristics patterned after Max Weber's bureaucratic model. Both of these features are often lacking in the bureaucracies of developing countries. Even when they are formally present, in practice, the bureaucrats ignore them. Chapter five discusses how difficult it is for public policies to be implemented in the Third World. Although other problems are mentioned, the focus in the chapter is on these two previously identified ones. In addition to these two problems, the chapter also directs attention to two other features of the public policy environment which have a major influence on how implementation is to proceed: a) the constraints on policy implementation that may be part and parcel of foreign aid, and b) the availability of trained personnel. These two factors are as pivotal in shaping implementation as decentralization/centralization and adherence to Weberian norms.

4

Risks and Conflicts in Centralized State Intervention in Development Organizations

In developing countries, the management of development is usually concentrated in the public sector. Government economic development strategies place great power in the centralized national bureaucracies, which are sometime heavily dominated by incompetent and/or corrupt officials. In other cases, the inadequacy of the central government administrative structures complicates the task of project management. This chapter highlights the various administrative and political risks involved when bilateral and/or multilateral donors try to circumvent the many obstacles created by state intervention and suggests new approaches to development project management to minimize the conflicts between donor organizations and recipient countries organizations.

Development is a continuing process of mutually related economic, social, and political changes in a society. It is a process of applying new knowledge, techniques, and equipment to improve the standard of living of members of a community. Its ultimate purpose is to provide opportunities for a better life to all sections of the population.

Development also paves the way for another, more subtle process, namely modernization. The two terms are sometimes used interchangeably. Both generally signify societal transformations that give effect to a complex web of social, economic, and political changes. However, development is a term that should be defined differently for each country. The idea that it ought to transform an agricultural economy into a highly industrialized one is totally inadequate for some very small countries. These countries should conceive of national development in terms of achievement of certain goals, associated with the welfare of their populations, attained through the maximum utilization of their resources, land, labor, etc.

Interestingly enough, the bureaucrats of many developing countries were the vocal supporters of a dependency approach. They originally questioned why capitalist development, such as had occurred in the United States and other Western countries, had no taken place in the developing countries. In their efforts to obtain more and more foreign aid, they deliberately presented an image of being unable to cope by themselves with the tasks of development. Lacking in funding and strategies for responding to this challenge, international donors have limited their actions to timid innovations introduced through projects in different sectors of the economy of these countries.

There are many different analysis on the effects of foreign aid and the activities of international organizations in the less developed countries (LDCs). The discussion on a higher effectiveness of aid, however, has to involve a reflection of the structure and the performance of various bureaucracies on both the donors and the recipients side — the multilateral and bilateral aid agencies on one hand, and the public administrations in LDCs on the other.

While the first group of administrations has been constantly under criticism over the past years (i.e. The United States interventions on the budgets and organizational reforms inside the Food Agricultural Organization (FAO), United Nations Education, Scientific, and Cultural Organization (UNESCO), United Nations (UN), Organization of American States (OAS), etc.), the discussion on a higher performance of recipient countries' bureaucracies is nowadays closely related to a new type of international cooperation, i.e. structural adjustment policies. International organizations claim that the channeling of resources is one activity, which could only be effectively pursued if recipient countries' structures are reformed. There is no need to channel more resources towards countries where the overall structure of, for example, the financial system (i.e. negative interest rates) is more likely to favor higher income groups and large firms more than the lower income groups in the urban and rural areas. Given such structures, the effectiveness and sustainability of even "perfectly" identified, evaluated and designed development projects would be limited.

Sectoral and structural adjustment policies would be one way to improve sectoral development in LDCs economies as well as the overall performance of the public sector. The governments' administrative capacity will be crucial to their ability to organize and carry out programs of economic reforms. Unfortunately in most developing countries, the bureaucracy forms an influential interest group that may oppose structural reforms and stabilization.

Administrative as well as economic reform often requires reducing the size of the public sector through government employee layoffs and careful privatization of public enterprises. Such policies are at odds with the interests of many bureaucrats, especially the higher officials who may lose influence by these reforms. Most African and Latin American studies on elite-behavior show that there are very close links between public administrators and urban/rural elites. They closely work together for common interests. This is very clearly analyzed for Brazil which is a far more advanced LDC (Garcia-Zamor 1978), also for Haiti (Garcia-Zamor 1986). These traditional elites are an effective block against a broader development of a market economy, especially by excluding rural transformations towards a more equitable distribution of lands. They live very well with a limited market economy where high ranking administrators and managers of the public sector as well as private managers, technicians and entrepreneurs all share the fruits of their export sector by appropriating rents. Most governments have additionally easy access to the central bank's resources, which are very frequently filled with foreign aid and external resources. It is well known that poor countries often have rich elites. Given this interest block, most small entrepreneurs have very restricted possibilities of independent production and distribution, and public administration is frequently seen as "belonging to the other" by the underprivileged. Since international organizations and bilateral aid agencies give the most important impulses towards promoting these groups of small producers that are not represented in the public sector's agencies, conflicts often develop between donor and recipient bureaucracies.

Even more upsetting to external assistance agencies is the fact that the behavior of the economic and bureaucratic elites helps limit the expansion of market forces and of a market economy. Underdeveloped capitalism has led to a majority of dispersed and isolated producers with very weak associations and interest organizations. There is hardly an effective representation of workers, in the sense of a broad representation of rural and urban workers, the unemployed and underemployed. These unions, and especially the leading union representatives, are closely linked to the state apparatus by clientelistic ties or corruptive practices. Due to an "underdeveloped" industrial sector, this faction of the society is too small, and strikes usually benefit a worker's aristocracy (i.e.. The Mexican unions). Those strikes may be a paralyzing part of the economy for some days, but usually strikes do not have transformation capacity and usually do not involve underemployed and unemployed workers. Given these weak structures "from below," there actually seems to exist no ability to put more pressure on the bureaucracy towards a more responsible form of identification and implementation of public policies and development projects.

There are, however, some limited chances for adjusting public administration in developing countries by some kind of "pressure from below." In recent years there has been a concerted effort by many donor organizations to involve recipients in the planning and management of projects (Garcia-Zamor 1985). Perhaps a combination of "external pressure" and "pressure from below" may lead to a new sharpening of the public sector and an improvement of its policy making capacity. The actual budgetary crisis of some donor agencies is already stimulating the discussion of reforming/strengthening public sector management.

In the late 1980's, the House Foreign Affairs Committee of the United States Congress had formed a bipartisan Task Force on foreign assistance for a broad review of the entire U.S. assistance program. The purpose of the Task Force review was threefold:

- To identify and assess major problems in U.S. foreign assistance programs;
- To define more precisely its objectives; and
- To try to strengthen those programs that can enhance U.S. national interest.

With the onset of Gramm-Rudman budget constraints, fiscal year 1988 signaled the first major cutbacks in the U.S. foreign aid program after six years of major increases. In the eve of the new millennium, the United States is facing the problem of rising expectations among foreign assistance recipients, and must decide what relatively few countries will receive the bulk of the funding.

In a 1988 report, the chairman of the United States Congress Task Force criticized the U.S. Agency for International Development (USAID) as an organization spending too much time planning and justifying what it is doing, and not enough time on implementing projects and determining their impact. Because of the pressure (partly from Congress itself) for financial accountability, USAID employees sometime sit at word processors rather than work in the field, a process that may keep USAID honest but also keeps them from the development process. (Hamilton 1988). The Task Force strongly recommended a policy dialogue between the United States and recipient countries while being tolerant of the problems involved in addressing development and economic issues. However, such a dialogue might be often difficult since the United States might want to avoid pumping resources into recipient countries with ineffective, even disastrous economic policies. However, a large portion of the economic assistance program is in the form of military assistance which provides weapons and defense services to friendly foreign countries on a grant basis. At the beginning of the Reagan administration, this form of assistance was $110 million. By 1987, it was $950 million. For example, at the onset of the Reagan administration, military assistance to Spain was about $150 million a year. By 1985, Spain was receiving $400 million a year. Military aid to Turkey was about $ 250 million, but by 1985 had reached about $700 million. Portugal received $52.8 million in military aid, but in 1985 received $128 million. Greece received $180 million but by 1985 was receiving about $500 million. Comparing the 1978 foreign assistance program with the 1987 program, military assistance increased from 26 percent to 36 percent of the entire programs while resources devoted to development assistance declined from 21 percent of the total to 15 percent and food assistance declined from 14 percent to 10 percent (Hamilton 1988). While avoiding requirements that might be impossible to meet, most donors are under some kind of pressure to establish some conditionality tying aid and economic reforms.

Most of the conflicts that arise in the interactions between state centralized bureaucracies and donor organizations have originated because of one or more of the following factors:

The technical assistance is given often in form of projects that take place outside the immediate vicinity of the capitals. Donors have been trying over the years to get recipients involved in the planning and management of these projects (Garcia-Zamor 1985). Bureaucrats in the central governments who make most decisions without local consultations sometimes view this involvement negatively. The practice of "centralism" in many developing countries is a tradition inherited from their past colonial masters. The political situation before independence had blocked the development of a responsible and competent bureaucracy.

Donors tend sometime to tie development assistance to political reforms. Some of the suggested reforms are based on the Western model of democracy, which emphasizes "free elections." However, even in industrialized societies, voters have limited ability to affect policy, and that limited influence is tempered by the character of the dominant party system and the reigning political culture. In the United States, much scholarly opinion does not attribute important political or policy consequences to the constriction of the electorate. In fact, a fair amount of academic work has been directed to explain why non-voting should not be considered a problem at all (Piven and Richard 1988: 9 and 13.) Furthermore, the mere participation in the electoral process is no guarantee of meaningful participation. In Brazil, even during the years of military rule when most citizens were critical about the political system, nonvoting was at a record low. The reason was that a validated voter's participation card was required to obtain all vital government services.

The bloated public sector bureaucracies of most developing countries become a drain of resources. Some efforts have been made in several African countries to drastically reduce the size of the bureaucracies but their successes have been quite limited. (Garcia-Zamor 1987). In many cases, governments that are faced with massive unemployment problems and potential political unrest have chosen to use the public sector to create jobs. In Venezuela for example, thanks in part to a presidential decree requiring that every public bathroom and elevator have an attendant, public sector employment tripled from 1974-84.

A maze of government regulations and trade restrictions often benefit only politically connected companies and penalize entrepreneurs and consumers. Donor organizations try constantly to open the systems for a more even development of the economies. This is a source of constant conflict between the two parties.

Finally, there is often a lack of real desire for change at the top of the political leadership. Unfortunately many chiefs of government are either incompetent or corrupt. Whereas in large industrialized bureaucracies it is possible for a government to be headed by a president of limited intellectual ability, in small developing nations a mediocre president cannot work to develop the system. Too much is expected of the leader when other strong institutions are missing.

The only way to bring administration and policy implementation to a higher efficiency is to have a broader economic participation by careful re-privatization and deregulation. Of course, this should go hand in hand with some kind of political participation where elections are held at the different levels of government. As far as development policies are concerned, this idea leads to the realization that the possibilities of international cooperation and the role of foreign aid are limited. Many years of empirical observation of the bureaucracies of Africa and Latin America have shown a clear resistance to change behavior in policies of structural reform, especially when the primary beneficiaries of development projects were under-privileged producers and poverty groups.

5

THE APPLICATION OF
MAX WEBER'S MODEL
IN NON-WESTERN PUBLIC
BUREAUCRACIES

Successful policy implementation in developed societies has depended on two important features of the Western bureaucracies: their decentralized structure and their adherence to a set of characteristics patterned after Max Weber's bureaucratic model. Both of these features are often lacking in the bureaucracies of developing countries. Even when they are formally present, in practice they are ignored by the bureaucrats. This may appear to be a sweeping generalization since there is not sufficient similarity among so-called developed societies with regard to adherence to Weberian bureaucratic norms. Certainly there are very different structural patterns of policy implementation in unitary versus federal systems. Federally generated public policy in the United States tends to follow a fairly decentralized pattern. However, this is largely due to a) the federal system; b) a constitutional structure that intentionally fragments authority; and c) a politically active business sector that possesses a tremendous amount of informal veto power vis-a-vis decisions made by the federal government and/or the state governments. It cannot be said that governmental authority is similarly fragmented (and therefore decentralized) in France or the U.K. In addition, the United States federal bureaucracy contains a curious mixture of career bureaucrats (who presumably acquired their positions via merit) and politically appointed officials who serve at the pleasure of the chief executive. There is probably less administrative neutrality in the United States than there is in many European bureaucracies. The United States and Europe do not have the same administrative traditions and the Europeans have tended to develop a corps of professional civil servants where the Weberian bureaucratic norm of "administrative neutrality" is more deeply imbedded.

This chapter will discuss how difficult it is for public policies to be implemented in the Third World. Although other problems are mentioned, the focus in this chapter will be on the two identified in the previous paragraph. In addition to these two problems, the paper will also direct attention to two other features of the public policy environment which have some major influence on how implementation is to proceed: a) the constraints on policy implementation that may be part and parcel of foreign aid, and b) the availability of trained personnel. These two factors are as pivotal in shaping implementation as decentralization/centralization and adherence to Weberian norms. Like in the case of the developed societies, all developing countries are not alike. Therefore, it is difficult to offer empirical evidence that will apply to all of them. The basic proposition advanced in this chapter is a highly debatable one and is not equally applicable to all developing countries.

PROBLEMS OF PUBLIC POLICY FORMULATION

The ultimate goals of public policy are to improve the quality of future governmental decisions and to work toward improving the quality of some aspect of human life (Portney 1986). In view of this, public policy implementation is an important element in the developing countries' efforts to move forward. A crucial factor for implementation is the ability of public bureaucrats to identify all the variables which affect the achievements of their objectives (Mazmanian and Sabatier 1983: 21: Pressman and Wildavsky 1984). Implementation forges a casual goal between vague and sometimes conflicting policy objectives. Koeing states that:

Because policy goals are usually multiple, conflicting, and vague, and because of policy-makers' cognitive limitations and the unpredictable dynamics of the environment, it is impossible to anticipate all the relevant constraints applicable to a policy when it is adopted. Instead, they are discovered as implementation proceeds (Koeing 1986: 156).

A major obstacle to the achievement of developmental goals in the Third World is the inability of the public bureaucracies to formulate plans and to implement them properly. Even when innovative policies, inspired by foreign donors, are formulated, the ineffectiveness of the public servants in implementing them is an obstacle to the success of development assistance. As Bryant and White point out, "Administrative incapacity is often characterized by swollen bureaucracies encumbered with formalistic procedures that delay rather than expedite service delivery and program implementation" (Bryant and White 1982: 22). Contrary to the industrialized societies where public policy implementation involves countless, routine tasks by the public servants, in developing countries the ultimate goals of public policy implementation is the attainment of developmental objectives expressed in the national development plans. These plans are usually inspired by foreign donors and are based primarily on expected technical assistance from abroad. In addition, most developing countries do not have the administrative framework to handle the requirements imposed by donors of foreign aid.

ADMINISTRATIVE PREREQUISITES TO EFFECTIVENESS OF INTERNATIONAL ASSISTANCE

Many developing countries are now realizing that international development assistance is not going to solve their long-range problems. Many have reached that point where they have to pay more interest on past aid than they take in new aid. These countries incurred large debts in the 1970s because of the sharp increase in oil prices and now find it difficult to repay the loans because of depressed exports and low prices of their commodities. Most of them are asking the international banks to renegotiate their debts on easier terms. Figures published by the World Bank reveal that for the period from 1970 to 1985 the outstanding debt of oil-importing developing countries rose from $50.9 billion to $484.7 billion. During that same period the increase for the oil-exporting developing countries was from $17.7 billion to $226.5 billion. (World Bank 1986: 44). Since the late 1980's, most Developing countries were unable to obtain new net lending from private sources, except under rescheduling agreements. Negotiations for the rescheduling of existing debt in 1985 covered 19 World Bank members, including 10 from sub-Saharan Africa and seven from Latin America. In addition, many aid programs involved economic conditions that for a variety of reasons recipients would prefer to avoid. Furthermore, there was an increasing awareness that there was not a strong relationship between the amount of development assistance a country receives and its rate of development. Indeed some studies showed that aid correlates negatively with growth: those countries that have received the most aid also have had subsequently unimpressive growth rates.(Mende 1973: ch 7).

The 1980 report of the Independent Commission on International Development Issues, under the chairmanship of Willy Brandt, called for at least four billion dollars in aid over the next decades for the world's poorest countries. In addition, it called for an international system of universal revenue mobilization based on a sliding scale related to national income. The developed nations have shown little regard for the Brandt Report. As a matter of fact, most of the donor countries have reduced bilateral aid programs or kept them static. A few countries like Sweden and Canada have dramatically increased aid allocations, but these have not been adequate to compensate for lower commitments by the major countries. Furthermore, in the era of high inflation, high deficits, high unemployment of the late 1980's, and the seeming ingratitude of some developing nations, development assistance was not a politically popular issue for most of the traditional donor countries. The end result of the decreased assistance was a dramatic diminution of developing countries' capability to implement policies that were formulated without internally generated revenues for their realization.

But regardless of the form and the amount of development assistance that is given to the developing countries, a crucial factor for its effectiveness will still be the administrative capability of the bureaucracies of these countries to implement government policies. There is a need in almost all developing countries to establish or strengthen implementation capability to better manage the aid they receive. In general, the public servants in the developing countries lack administrative ability and managerial skill. Goodman and Love argued that intensive project investment in developing countries has failed to anticipate the impact on development goals for two reasons: 1) the lack of viable policies, coupled with poor management, has wasted valuable resources which led to counterproductive disharmony and tension; and 2) planning and project development take place within a social and economic environment which molds and limits the actions of implementing agencies (Goodman and Love 1979: xii).

The international lending institutions should rethink their policies and try to tie loans to countries' administrative environments because good projects and poor policy formulation and implementation do not make sense. Therefore, there is a need to do more administrative capability assessment prior to loan approval and/or disbursement. The pressure on developing countries to develop project formulation has not always taken the total administrative environment into consideration. In addition, two of the major lending institutions, the World Bank and the International Monetary Fund (IMF), often work at cross purposes. The reason: the World Bank's bias is for development, the IMF's for financial stabilization. The result: the developing countries are caught between two competing bureaucracies.

Usually changes occur in a policy during implementation. Berman differentiates between programmed and adoptive implementation, arguing that only under certain limited conditions should expected policies remain static during implementation (1980). For implementation to be successful, the goals of policies must be clearly and realistically stated. The problem with the implementation of policies in developing countries arises because policy-makers make unrealistic assumptions about their administrative processes. This almost invariably requires many adjustments in the policies during the process of implementation. Jones views implementation as a process of interaction between the setting of goals and the actions geared to achieving them (Jones 1984: 165). However, such necessary interaction is often inhibited in developing countries because of the fragmented nature of the bureaucracy. There is often an absence of adequate horizontal integration between its units.

AMBIVALENCE CONCERNING DECENTRALIZATION

As mentioned earlier, a major problem of policy implementation in developing countries is the centralization and fragmentation of their administrative structures. While the United States is moving rapidly into a "post-literary" condition, a condition where reading and writing have been displaced by television and video as the primary sources of mass entertainment and communication, most developing countries are still coping with a "preliterary" situation (Brumback 1988). In Brazil, one of the most advanced developing countries, for example, the findings of a research conducted in the late 1970's revealed that 12 percent of the Brazilian civil servants never went to school; 21 percent did not finish elementary school; 13 percent went to junior high school but did not graduate; 15 percent graduated from junior high; 13 percent attended a university, but only 2 percent received a university diploma (Garcia-Zamor 1978: 469-81). Unfortunately, this situation has not changed dramatically since then. The low level of formal education of civil servants in developing countries' is partly responsible for the excessive centralization of authority in the top echelons of their administrative structures (Garcia-Zamor 1986: 63-91). But the tendency to centralize administration is also a function of: 1) the governments' perceived need to control; 2) their lack of trust of lower level officials; and 3) perhaps a residual of colonial administration practice.

In the case of Nigeria, Cohen found out that typically the person heading an office or a department hands out very limited and partial tasks to subordinates. All coordination, planning, supervision and decision-making go to the center or top person in the department. Cohen attributed these features of over-centralization and excessive hierarchy to post-colonial functionalism (Cohen 1980).

Cheena and Rondinelli define decentralization as possessing four major forms: deconcentration; delegation to semi-autonomous or parastatal agencies; devolution to local governments; and transfer from public to non-governmental institutions. The two authors illustrate the ambivalence of developing nations concerning decentralization. First, although local governments were delegated "broad powers to perform development planning and management functions," adequate financial resources and qualified personnel to carry them out were often withheld." Second, they observed that local government officials are often reluctant to act independently. They continue to depend on the central government ministry officials for decisions (Cheena and Rondinelli 1983: 20 and 27).

But in the often informal setting of the developing countries, some degree of implementation initiative can exist even when the administrative structure itself is centralized. Esman observed that:

> The style of administration [in the developing world] involves changes within bureaucracy — away from hierarchical command and towards patterns that permit greater initiative and discretion at operating levels — and in relationships between administrators and clients in shaping programs of action that accommodate the objectives of government to clientele needs. In the assistance and guidance role, the administrator is a teacher, experimenter, the negotiator as well as a technician. These new patterns of interaction with clients are a hallmark that was not contemplated in the highly structured efficiency-oriented models of Western administration (Esman 1974: 14).

The degree of administrative discretion mentioned by Esman is clearly a non-Weberian pattern of behavior which can prevail in some cases even when the administrative structures are formally centralized. Kenye mentioned the negative consequences of excessive regulations (through centralization and/or control) when accompanied by uncontrolled implementation:

> Planned development in the third World has increased government intervention in the socio-economic sphere and this, in turn, has led to an increased number of regulations. These excessive regulations coupled with greater administrative discretion provide opportunities for corruption, since the regulations can be used to frustrate the public and result in bribery to avoid such frustrations (Kenye 1985).

In the same vein, Gould and Amaro-Reyes view centralization as one of the factors that encourage bureaucratic corruption in developing countries. They argue that the rigidity of overcentralized decision-making structures and processes tends to delay official action, focusing those seeking to expedite transactions to resort to bribes and payoffs as a means of overcoming cumbersome policy implementation procedures (Gould and Amaro-Reyes 1983: 14).

Harris states that politicians in most of the developing nations frequently make important policy decisions without the advice of their civil servants. Moreover, political leaders and party officials interfere to an excessive degree in even the detailed implementation of government policies and programs because of their lack of confidence in the loyalty of the bureaucrats. Harris thinks that party leaders in West Africa are often suspicious of the sympathies and values of the senior civil servants and he attributes this suspicion largely to differences in educational, social, or ethnic backgrounds (Harris 1965: 309).

The cost of failed policies has always hindered the action of bureaucrats both in developed and developing countries. In the United States the consequences of failure of policy formulation may be personal. The rule used to be that U.S. government employees could not be held personally liable for anything that happened while carrying out official duties, even if they were negligent in the way they did their job. While civil servants may have been sued, they rarely faced any serious consequences. However, in early 1988, the U.S. Supreme Court changed the rules to make civil servants more vulnerable to personal damage suits. That lack of immunity would have put government officials in the precarious situation of having to make policy decisions while worrying about placing their personal fortunes on the line. In a country where law suits are so commonplace, civil servants would worry about losing their homes and their savings. Top officials, with even more to lose personally, also will fret that their subordinates would hesitate about making decisions. However, a subsequent judicial measure gave relief to U.S. civil servants by stipulating any time a plaintiff has a complaint against a federal employee for some action taken as part of his or her job, the mechanism of the Federal Tort Claims Act come into play. That means first trying to settle the matter out of court and then suing the United States directly.

Bryant states that if one wants to maximize equity, decentralization may not be the best administrative route since locally entrenched elites are more ready to claim policy outputs than the lower income groups (1976: 47-48). There might be other advantages to centralization in developing countries. An obvious one is the elimination of the discretionary lapse between policy formulation and policy implementation. Policy-makers have a greater awareness, and sometimes even participate in the process of implementation. In the centralized systems of developing countries policies are more specific. Plans for implementation are less complicated when clear, unequivocal statements of the decisions regarding policy ends and means are formulated as a basis and stimulus for action. These usually entail precise decisions about objectives. The level of specificity is often impaired by the lack of knowledge of the relevant issues and facts by the civil servants who implement the policies. Contrary to what happens in developed countries where the complexity of the systems keeps policy-making in a very broad context, the developing countries try to eliminate from the start all problems and obstacles that may hinder achievement of the policy objectives. The interrelationships between policies and budgeting and the role of budgeting in policy implementation are more clearly delineated in developing countries. Accurate forecasts are usually used and the budgeting system is closely linked to policy formulation so that it serves as an effective instrument of implementation. Because of their lack of large resources and revenues, or in some cases because of pressures from international donors, developing countries tend to develop their budgets on the basis of specific policies. It could be said that 90 percent of all policies are really made at the time the national budget is being elaborated.

This rarely happens in large developed societies where administrative discretion often tries to adapt policies to local means. There, successful implementation occurs in an evolutionary way. The somewhat vague goals stated in policies are interpreted by administrators in various ways as they make their way down the organizational hierarchy. At the end of the process what actually is implemented could be quite different from the original policy and in some cases at variance with it.

In most developing countries, the lack of computers accounts for the existence of so many forms to be arduously filled out and approved by countless employees in every dealing with the bureaucracy. Countless signatures are needed on many routine procedures, a fact which delays administrative action and creates so much extra trivial work on the periphery of power that relatively little time remains for the execution of the broader tasks of public policy making. Because of the lack of adequate computers, the bureaucracies of developing countries are infested with tons of worthless documents which keep public employees more busy with paper than with people. In such a context, public policies often are made in response to red-tape instead of to people's needs. However, this is not particular to developing countries. Kaufman makes the same observation about the American bureaucracy (Kaufman 1977).

The introduction of systems analysis and computers in the public services of developing countries can also create obstacles to policy implementation. Many of these countries acquire computers only to find that their effective use depends upon rationalization of administrative processes, availability of data, and meaningful integration of data. The steps to improve information gathering and analysis capabilities require the establishment or strengthening of central statistical offices, improvement of data collection techniques and moves toward improvement of the quality of data.

DISTORTION OF THE WEBERIAN MODEL

Another major impediment to public policy implementation in developing countries is the distortion of the Weberian model of bureaucracy. One may argue that such distortion is understandable and even necessary, since Weber's model is clearly a formalistic one that lacks such dimensions as informal lines of authority and communication or concern for the individual worker in the bureaucracy. Weber himself indicated that his model was not meant to apply to all conceivable organizational situations, and that it represented only a broad framework rather than an all-encompassing model complete in every detail (Gordon 1986: 185). But developing countries tend to be more resistant to changes. They view Max Weber's bureaucratic model as the most perfected, rational means for framing and controlling human activity. However, with changes taking place in the technological, cultural, social and economic environment, the model is showing an ever-increasing number of imperfections and gaps. Although criticized, modified or only partly adapted, it has nonetheless served as a quasi-general reference for developing countries. But their bureaucracies have not been capable of integrating the necessary changes adapting it to their particular situation. In addition, it is difficult to assess when this espousal of the Weberian concept is sincere or simply motivated by self-serving circumstances. An African scholar, Bediako Lamouse-Smith, clearly made this point:

> The idea of an impartial public service and servants can be counted among the myths of the Weberian ideal type of bureaucracy. Yet in the post-independence civil services of Africa, one frequently meets complaints, especially from top officials, that the impartiality of the civil service is being tampered with by the new political leaders. I would suggest that the real meaning behind this complaint is that when the civil servants feel threatened by the dynamism of the imaginative politician, the concept of impartiality becomes a useful channel of escape (Lamouse-Smith 1974: 143).

O.P. Dwivedi expressed the same doubts about the Weberian approach in developing countries. He stated that while these countries continued to profess such administrative values as the doctrine of ministerial responsibility, political neutrality and anonymity of public servants, and the merit principles in recruitment and promotion, political leaders found that these values were counter-productive if the goal was acceleration of social and economic reforms. He stated further that when conflicts arise between inherited administrative values (Weber's model) and ends and means used by politicians, politics would emerge as the most important value in the governing of a nation (Dwivedi 1985). This is especially true in the case of small countries where social pressures could make an outcast of any public servant who tries to behave in an impersonal manner in the performance of his official duties. Price found out that in Ghana, the bureaucrat is expected to behave impartially when he is dealing with members of his extended kinship family in the bureaucratic setting but at the same time is expected to use his office in a manner that will enhance the wealth, status and influence of his group (Price 1975). Furthermore, in many developing countries the primary role of the bureaucracy is to serve and sustain the existing political system. Despite some degree of formal decentralization, there is very little delegation of authority. Usually the hierarchical structures exist only in the organizational charts. But in practice, instead of the formal organization pictured in the charts, the bureaucracy in the developing countries functions as an informal organization.

Usually in such instances, the bureaucracy is multifunctional. This multifunctionalism tends to cause overlapping of duties in various structures, and not enough specific knowledge of the various problems and possible solutions. On the positive side, multifunctionalism may promote the relative ease of public policy formulation and implementation. The distance from the administrative elite to the lowest bureaucratic official will not seem insurmountable. Communication from one level to the next is more easily accomplished than in the unifunctional Weberian bureaucracy. When the two major obstacles to policy implementation — overcentralization and the distortion of the Weberian model of bureaucracy — diminish, the individual bureaucrat has the opportunity to observe first hand the effects of any administrative decision which he makes. As a result, he is able to perform more effectively and to participate in the development of policy as well as in its implementation. For the bureaucrat so involved, this reduces the frustration which comes from the implementation of a policy which has been formulated without reference to his expertise.

It could be safely assumed that in most developing countries the two obstacles to public policy implementation, overcentralization and the anamorphosis of the Weberian bureaucratic model, are commonly accepted features of the bureaucracy. Therefore, the ability of the developing countries to implement policies will be adversely affected by the degree of their adherence to these two characteristics, especially when accompanied by the usual constraints that come with foreign aid and the lack of trained personnel.

PART III

ETHICS AND DEVELOPMENT
IN LATIN AMERICA

The two chapters of Part III deal with Latin America. Despite sustained economic growth, Latin America harbors more poor people than ever before and the gap between poor and rich yawns wider. Tim Johnson provided statistics in a Miami Herald article of March 17, 1998 showing that some 150 million persons, roughly 33 percent of the total population of the region, currently live in conditions of extreme poverty. A Berlin-based organization to fight corruption, Transparency International, released in 1998 an index of public perception of corruption and five Latin American nations were ranked among the eleven most corrupt countries in the world. Larry Luxner, in a Miami Herald article of March 16, 1998, explained that corruption is the number one political issue in Latin America in 1998, attracting more attention from voters and the media than violent crime, poverty, or unemployment. This situation prompted the Organization of American States to adopt an Inter-American Convention Against Corruption on March 29 1996. Subsequently, several Latin American countries created National Offices of Public Ethics to enforce the preventive measures proposed by the convention.

However, violent crime, especially urban violence, has also become a grave problem in Latin America. According to Andres Oppenheimer, in a Miami Herald article of March 23, crime was so high in 1998 that the Inter-American Development Bank — normally dedicated to solving economic problems — gave out more than $80 million dollars loans to train police officers. The new loans mark a departure from the previous conventional wisdom among experts that urban violence could best be attacked by reducing poverty. Economists are beginning to look at urban violence as an economic catastrophe, much like earthquakes, droughts or floods. It is scaring away foreign and domestic investments, causing huge drops in tourism and forcing governments to spend a large amount of money on security and hospital bills. Urban violence and corruption have become part of Latin America's leading economic indicators.

Chapter six reviews the rich administrative ethics legacy of the region and draws some lessons for modern ethical development administration. The chapter reviews some aspects of the administrative systems of Latin America's three most ancient civilizations: the Aztecs, the Mayas and the Incas and discusses their lasting legacies to present-day public administration. It would be impractical to look at the ancient civilizations' policies and practices discussed in the chapter as currently applicable models, but some modern national administrations, especially in the Third World, could be inspired by them. They were very rational, and their bureaucratic tasks were meticulously designed and efficiently enforced. Their efficiency consisted not only of technical competence but of attitudes and behavioral approaches that were, for their time and place, humane.

Although the civilizations of the Aztecs, Incas, and Mayas were not preoccupied with the process of development as a vital instrument for their survival, their own notions of "nation-building" and "institution building" were not very different from those of present day developing nations. They were able to develop some monumental projects without the assistance of the outside world. Although the three civilizations considered here extended for several centuries and, therefore, had different priority policies and activities at different stages of their respective development, sufficient evidence of extended administrative practices is available to make them highly relevant to contemporary public administration.

One of the administrative ethics prescription recommended at the end of Chapter three was ethical training. Chapter seven places emphasis on how such training should be planned. Since many of the courses that are offered in Latin America are designed in more developed countries, the courses often fail to take into consideration the administrative, cultural, socio-economic, and political peculiarities of the countries. The first problem that trainers face is that many Latin American public servants come to the training dogmatically committed to a moral relativism that offers them no grounds to think that even minor ethical violations in the work place are just plainly wrong. Of course, each Latin American country is different from the others. The question can even be raised about whether there are common values within the same country and culture. All cultures have a concept of good and bad, but what is good and bad vary widely from one cultural group to another. Two countries, Guatemala and Mexico, are used as case studies to show the application of the model.

6

LATIN AMERICAN
ANCIENT CIVILIZATIONS
AND THEIR
ADMINISTRATIVE LEGACIES

This chapter reviews some aspects of the administrative systems of Latin America's three most ancient civilizations: the Aztecs, the Mayas and the Incas and discusses their lasting legacies to present-day public administration. It would be impractical to look at the ancient civilizations' policies and practices discussed in this chapter as current applicable models, but some modern national administrations, especially in Latin America, could be inspired by them. They were very rational and their bureaucratic tasks were meticulously designed and efficiently enforced. Although the contemporary ethical theories discussed in the previous two chapters were constantly violated in favor of good and productive practices, their efficiency consisted not only of technical competence but of attitudes and behavioral approaches that were, for their time and place, humane.

Despite the fact that the civilizations of the Aztecs, Incas, and Mayas were not preoccupied with the process of development as a vital instrument for their survival, their own notions of "nation-building" and "institutions building" were not very different from those of present day developing nations. They were able to develop some monumental projects without the assistance of the outside world. Although the three civilizations considered here extended for several centuries and therefore had different priority policies and activities at different stages of their respective development, sufficient evidence of extended administrative practices is available to make them very relevant to contemporary development administration.

The chapter reviews specifically the following five major administrative problems that the ancient civilizations faced and discusses how the solutions that were found for them could serve as a model for contemporary public administration:

- Unorganized and inefficient bureaucracy
- Inadequate and unfair tax collection system
- Nugatory agricultural practices
- A warped judicial order
- A poor educational system

UNORGANIZED AND INEFFICIENT BUREAUCRACY

Good administration is a term that should be defined differently for each country and for each time period. Any definition of good and efficient administration should include the achievement of specific objectives through the management of a bureaucracy. Although the objectives of the rulers of the ancient civilizations were sometimes different from those of contemporary governments, these rulers managed their bureaucracies effectively, often mixing both democratic and despotic methods no longer acceptable. A brief review of their administrative machineries follows.

The Aztecs

The main objective of Aztec public policy was to make alliances and form and administer an empire. The Aztecs excelled in administration. Their growing empire was governed more efficiently than many contemporary nations. The social system made each person feel that he or she played a vital part. Most questions of life or death were answered for the commoner by a combination of priests, warriors, statesmen, scientists, and teachers that could handle any eventuality (Peterson 1979:104). The tasks of service delivery of the Aztec bureaucracy was simplified by grouping families within the tribes to form "divisions" for the purposes of land distribution and exploitation. No one was permitted to own land. In addition to deciding when the land should be cultivated and on which days the crops were to be reaped, these "divisions" had higher administrative and military duties. Each was an organization having its own headman and council. These "divisions" were named Calpulli. Their most important duty was the redistribution of land which occurred, at most, once every four years. Women held no office in this male-dominated society. Nevertheless, they advised their husband and sons, and so were able to exert a considerable unofficial pressure (Burland and Forman 1985:73).

The Mayas

The ancient Maya was not a theocracy or primitive democracy, but rather a class society with strong political power concentrated in a hereditary elite. The Mayas had an excellent method of formalized territorial organization. Eventually some of the larger centers achieved a status approaching urban cities. For example, at Tikal, hundreds of structures believed to be residences of persons other than peasant farmers were mapped within the city's central precincts. No doubt the existence of this diversified social organization also brought about complex administrative problems necessitating a host of civil servants (magistrates, tribute collectors, law enforcers, etc.) who, along with the artists, craftsmen, merchants, almost surely constituted the equivalent of a "middle class" (Gallenkamp 1976:110). Occasionally peasants might have been employed in the lower levels of this bureaucracy or filled certain posts on a rotating basis, with positions of authority periodically changing, allowing adult males to work their way up a hierarchy ladder by holding a series of increasingly prestigious offices.

There is abundant evidence that the Mayan bureaucrats combined religious with civil functions. Religion was of central importance in Mayan life, and authority was exercised by a closely co-operating group of priests, each of whom acted equally as a leader over a particular geographical area. Some formal method of control must be assumed to account for the stable and orderly character of Mayan civilization over so wide an area and for so long a period of time (Morley and Brainerd 1983: 437). The "official" image which emerges from Mayan documents is one of a static, caste-bound society; it is a world of the ruling classes, whom the people support and maintain in exchange for a completely abstract prosperity, made up of prophecies, mysteries, and collective mysticism. Very little social tension existed: only religious activity and great building enterprises (Calvani 1976: 88).

The Incas

The Incas were masters of organization. They turned conquest into empire. In a land where for geographical, topographical, hydrographical and economic reasons, tight planning of resources was required, the Incas were extremely efficient. Their bureaucracy excelled in service delivery. The production and distribution of food, clothing and services, including road and canal building, were all functions of the state. The Incas had an effective way of securing a loyal civil service. It was provided by a sort of formalized and licit nepotism. They also created an administrative machine capable of dealing with the vast territory under their control. The Incas tried to have provinces correspond as much as possible to the native kingdoms they had added to the empire, or to tribal groups. However, when these were too small to fit the Inca notion of administrative efficiency, they combined two or three of them to constitute a province. To the Incas, a province was a certain number of taxpayers, neatly fitted into a decimal system. The top taxpaying unit consisted of ten thousand persons and, to be recognized as a province, a territory had to have at least one such unit. Most provinces had between two and four such units (Karen 1975: 97). Provincial governors were carefully selected and their positions were

appointments by merit, not by heredity as in the civil service. Thus, the Incas did not merely conquer foreign tribes and kingdoms with their armies; their administrative leadership peacefully integrated these people into one cohesive and viable political unit.

A magnificent system of Incan-built roads linked the heart of the empire, Cusco, with the most distant provinces (Martin 1974: 10). Through the matchlessly logical administrative hierarchy which, since the days of the earlier Incas, had gradually grown to amazing efficacy, society was firmly welded vertically to the person of the ruler. The gravest lack of the Incaic system lay in the complete absence of horizontal bonds linking officials of equal rank.

The flow of authority was ever from the top down through the orderly sequence of ranks to the lowest officials (Means 1964: 10-11). An extraordinary efficient postal service permitted dispatches to circulate rapidly. Messengers were stationed on major roads. They lived in groups of four or six in two thatched huts located about a mile from each other. The messengers were all young men who were especially good runners, and it was their duty to keep permanent watch of the road in order to catch sight of messengers from the other relays, and hurry out to meet them. To enable them to do this, these huts were built on high ground, in sight of one another (Vega 1961: 157).

Bureaucrats were required to furnish their superiors with a record of births and deaths that had occurred in the territories they administered. Thanks to this constant census of his subjects, which was carried out kingdom by kingdom and province by province, the Inca ruler was able to make a judicious distribution of the tasks necessary to the public welfare. He also prepared an annual report on what each province produced in the way of goods. This was in order to learn what provisions would be required to come to the assistance of his vassals in the event they were to suffer from shortages or had a poor harvest, including what quantities of wool and cotton that would be needed to clothe them (Vega 1961: 22).

INADEQUATE AND UNFAIR
TAX COLLECTION SYSTEM

Most contemporary developing countries lack an adequate and fair tax collection system. A fair tax would be one that treats equally people in equal economic circumstances. This is known as horizontal equity. But a fair tax should also treat people in unequal economic situation unequally. This is vertical equity. The ideal is that taxes should be distributed among taxpayers in relation to their ability to pay. State revenues based on tax collection are low because, even when a collection system exists, there are no serious consequences for those who evade payment. Government of most developing countries continue to base their development plans on expected foreign assistance and put little energy into generating internal revenues. These governments can learn in this area from the ancient civilizations. All of them had very efficient tax collection systems and the revenue collected (in form of consumer goods since they had no money economy) was judiciously used to promote the welfare of their people.

The Aztecs

Montezuma's empire comprised approximately thirty provinces, each with a central town for collecting tribute, and many with governors imposed to facilitate exploitation. The tribute exacted from these provinces sustained the government, the officials, the educational system, state granaries for emergencies, and rewards for deserving warriors. Power was concentrated at the top. The Aztecs had a dictatorship and a political centralization based on an imperial type of hierarchy. Their tribute system was administered by an autocratic bureaucracy (Peterson 1979: 116). Continuity of payment was enforced by tax-gathering officials in key places; if their demands were not met, a military expedition was undertaken and the exactions greatly increased (Davies 1973: 110). At the time of the Spanish Conquest, the annual tribute collected by the ruler included no less than 52,000 tons of foodstuffs, 123,400 cotton garments and 33,860 bundles of feathers. This tribute in kind was only a part of what the provinces contributed. In addition, services were extracted in the form of labor to build Montezuma's pyramid and other buildings. The frontier areas where supplies were provided for war were often exempted from paying taxes (Vega 1961: 112).

The Mayas

It would have been difficult for such a compact and well organized society as the Maya to flourish without a strong social hierarchy battening upon it. Each Mayan village or settlement came under the control of a Lord, to whom taxes were payable. These taxes were twofold: on produce, and in personal service. A portion of all crops harvested had to be paid over to the state. These crops were stored in warehouses and later distributed to the non-productive members of society (Whitlock 1976: 67). To assist in governing outlying villages, magistrates known as batab (ax bearers) were selected. Essentially they functioned as provincial mayors, keeping a close rein on local government, judicial matters, and overseeing the collection of tributes paid by the peasants to the hierarchy. As with the Aztecs, the tribute also included produce, a kind of woven cotton cloth called pati, domesticated fowls, salt, dried fish, and all kinds of game and birds. It also included cacao, copal for incense, honey and wax, strings of jade and coral beads, and shells (Morley and Brainerd 1983: 218).

The Incas

The Incas used personal service as a form of taxation, and agricultural work became the economic basis of the system. Each family cultivated not only its own plot of land, but also worked on the fields and was assigned to a state farm that supported the political superstructure (Bennett and Bird 1949: 221). In return for their fixed and reasonable share of the national product, the Inca upper caste provided sound and reliable administration, justice, welfare services, military services, and religious services. Everyone was provided with clothing, shoes, food, and all that is necessary in life, and it may be said there was no poor man or beggar throughout the Empire. But while there were no poor, there were no rich either, since everyone had what was necessary without living in luxury (Vega 1961: 125). It is safe to say that a high proportion of the architectural and technological constructions built in the Incaic period, temples, storehouse, roads, tambos (inns), bridges, fortresses, reservoirs, irrigation ditches, agricultural terraces, etc., was dedicated to the direct or indirect benefit of the people rather than to the selfish vanity of the rulers (Means 1964: 11). Money was unknown and the myriad of evil, avarice, corruption, cruelty, and oppression, which follows in its train were less present. Value alone was known, value in the form of flocks, utensils, apparel, food, drink, shelter, materials for handicrafts, and these came in abundance to all who would work for them diligently (Ibid).

NUGATORY AGRICULTURAL PRACTICES

In most developing countries agriculture is the main source for accumulating savings. Agricultural practices are thus vital for the overall development process. Public efforts to advance the agricultural progress in developing countries in Asia and the Far East are noticeable. However, in most Latin American and African countries the relationship between agricultural development and the total development process has not been clearly recognized. Despite rapid urbanization, the population in most developing areas is still concentrated in rural areas or small towns. Archaic political structures and outlooks tend to prevail in the rural areas, resisting changes which could raise production and permit broader distribution of benefits. An industrialization strategy is almost an inevitable phenomenon in the developing countries because their bureaucracies view it as the most reliable way toward development. However, instead of using the agricultural sector to provide raw materials for their new industries, they often fail to integrate that sector in their industrialization strategy. Furthermore, economic development usually brings a relative, if not an absolute, decline in the agricultural labor force.

The following brief review of agricultural practices in the ancient civilizations of Latin America shows that one key factor in the successful utilization of the land was the rulers' ability to mount major agricultural works programs, to whose implementation the entire peasantry was fully committed. These agricultural works programs transformed traditional practices into "modern" ones in order to increase production.

The Aztecs

As mentioned earlier, the most important duty of Calpulli was the redistribution of land, which occurred at least every four years. The cultivated area, which had been worked until there were signs of declining yield, was burnt over. The other areas which had been left uncultivated for some eight years were then divided. The plots allocated to families were scattered about in the whole section of land. This was a wise provision, because it meant that everyone had an equal chance of farming a plot of richer land (Burland and Forman 1985: 73-74).

After receiving the land, they began the spring sowing. The women and the children usually helped in this task. Very few Aztecs practiced any kind of irrigation, although they did fertilize their fields. The result of this system of land distribution and exploitation was that everyone accumulated a basic amount of food that could probably see the entire society through difficult times. The farmer was thus the support of the nation (Ibid.: 75).

The Mayas

Fundamental to the great achievements of the Maya people was the rare quality of knowing how to organize themselves to work as a team. Rarely in his life did a Maya act on his own or only for himself. This was particularly true in agriculture. The nature of the terrain was such that teams of peasants were needed to open up clearings in the forest, to cut down trees, to burn roots, and to keep clear the soil which had been sown laboriously (Calvari 1976: 59). Like the Aztecs, the Mayans depended on farmers. Rulers collected and distributed food surpluses. On occasion, political leaders extended their influence into the sphere of agriculture, particularly in the Late Classic period. In what is now called the Classic Period, from 250 to 900 A.D., the Mayas built some 200 cities in southern Mexico, Guatemala, and Belize and parts of Honduras and El Salvador. Places like Palenque, Tikal and Coplan, with their soaring pyramids, represent the splendors of the period, though more recent discoveries have revealed that the civilization was prospering in the southern low lands of Guatemala even centuries before. With increased specialization, administrative intervention was sometimes necessary to avoid the collapse of fragile economic systems in the face of crop failure or problems with the surplus of raw materials (Henderson 1981: 152).

In a Washington Post article of February 18, 1991, W. Booth wrote that some scholars believe that the Maya were diligent farmers of swamps. They piled up the muck from the bajos (seasonal swamps) and created raised gardens surrounded by culverts and drainage ditches. The muck from the swamp and ditches would then become fertile soil.

The ability to manage water lies at the center of vigorous debate over the rise and fall of the Maya. In much the same way that aggressive water management drew large populations to the arid landscape of Los Angeles and Phoenix, the Maya elite may have constructed elaborate systems to collect and store rainwater to draw settlers to their ceremonial centers.

Recently, a group of archaeologists working in Guatemala discovered a largely overlooked clever network of reservoirs and dams, stone-paved storm sewers and clay-lined drainage ditches that may have helped the Maya survive brutal bouts of seasonal drought. The management of water, the researchers say, could have been crucial in the creation of the powerful and advanced Maya nation-state.

The Incas

For administrative purposes the Incas divided the lands of the empire into three categories: the lands of the sun-god, the lands belonging to the Incan emperor and his imperial circles, and the lands that remained the communal property of the people. The people themselves were clustered into groups. The Incas clustered the heads of families into groups of ten, one hundred, five hundred, one thousand and ten thousand men and placed them under the direct authority of an Incan official whose rank in the Incan hierarchy depended on the number of individuals in his command. For example, a provincial governor had authority over forty thousand family heads. Imperial representatives, carefully instructed at court, periodically inspected all the subdivisions of the empire to audit accounts, revise policies, administer justice, and implement the emperor's directives (Martin 1974: 14).

A method was developed to rotate labor. Under this system, the commoners worked in turn the fields of the sun, the fields of the emperor, and the peasants' communal lands. The agricultural products of these communal lands were distributed among the commoners' households. The products yielded by the fields of the emperor and by the fields of the sun maintained the imperial court and the royal officials, fed and clothed those drafted into the Incan armies or into labor groups engaged in public works, and supported the priests and virgins consecrated to the cult of the sun. The surplus was stored in royal ganaries and warehouses to be distributed among the people in case of need (Ibid.).

The key factor in the Incas' success in agriculture was their skill in using water. Despite the height of the Andes and the absence of electricity, steam engines, dynamite and iron, they were able to build great reservoirs where the water was collected and released slowly into miles of canals constructed through the mountains. As soon as the Incas had conquered a new province, they immediately sent engineers there to build canals for irrigation. The management of irrigation water and the immense works associated with it must have required a special administrative department.

When the highland farmers ran short of arable land, they invented terracing, which not only gave them more room but checked erosion and runoff. In time, every valley was a spectacle of tier upon tier of terraces, with those at the float being perhaps a mile wide and those at the top, a few feet, and the range of crops varying in kind from the temperate-zone cultigens at the top down to the tropical-zone plants at the lower levels (Hyams and Ordish 1963: 25). This system is still being used in most developing countries to fight the erosion caused by intense deforestation and is the direct result of lessons already learned from ancient civilizations.

A WARPED JUDICIAL ORDER

The laws and their enforcement by judicial, quasi-judicial and administrative hierarchies have important implications with regard to administrative capabilities for economic and social development on the one hand and for human rights and welfare, on the other. In the developing countries, the judicial systems generally have serious deficiencies. For example, the laws on important subjects may be deficient or inadequate; people may not understand the laws; legal processes may be slow and ineffective; legal services may be out of the reach of some persons; and privileged individuals may see themselves above any law of the land.

Unfortunately the judicial system has not often been seen as a relevant factor when dealing with economic development. However, it has great capacity for facilitating change in many areas of the economy and the social order. Most particularly, a fair judicial system can provide a degree of certainty and predictability in economic relationships among individuals and, more importantly between governments and individuals.

A review of the judicial systems of the ancient civilizations of Latin America will follow. It will indicate how rulers were able to promote the development and welfare of their subjects using a legal framework that can still inspire progressive reforms in the judicial systems of developing countries.

The Aztecs

The administration of justice in the Aztec empire was something about which any nation could proudly boast, although the punishments were savage and vengeful. Because a criminal was liable not only to the society but to his gods as well, he was punished doubly. The laws of the Aztecs were an integral part of their life, reflecting their culture and mentality. Laws were equally applicable to high and low levels of society. However, the nobility and other privileged classes were judged by separate courts, and received private but more severe punishment (Peterson 1979: 118-121).

It should be pointed out that under Montezuma's rule, lawgiving was by no means confined to court etiquette and sumptuary rules; he promulgated, in addition, a new legal code governing such general matters as education, religious practices and festivities, while not ignoring such detailed questions as the treatment of adulterers, who were to be stoned and then thrown into a river.

Drunkenness was another capital offense. This provision was applied even more strictly to nobles than to commoners; the former were to be killed for a first offense, while the latter were given a second chance before being executed (Davies 1973: 109). This is an interesting contrast to some contemporary practices of forgiving effective leaders for their violation of ethical standards. Polls taken in the United States, for example, reveal that people there are very tolerant of their leaders' ethical lapses if the general economic condition of the country is good.

The Mayas

There are no records of a Mayan system of justice that was as disciplined as the Aztecs' one. For one thing, the method of any kind of law enforcement would have faced the problem of the huge area to be regimented. A major deterrent from the use of repressive government methods was the scattered nature of the population. This remarkably smooth running yet informal style of government must have depended upon a placid and well adjusted citizenry, who held a notable unanimous opinion as to proper behavior. Two authors, after observing this, quoted Lord Moulton as saying in a different context; "the measure of civilization is the extent of man's obedience to the unenforceable." In this criterion, they added, the Maya must have measured high (Morley and Brainerd 1983: 58).

The Incas

The leader of the smallest group of heads of households (usually number- ing ten families) had two principal responsibilities. One, more or less that of an attorney, or representative, consisted in diligently and earnestly soliciting the help of the higher authorities, on behalf of those under his jurisdiction who were in any sort of difficulty. The second responsibility, which was of a judicial nature, consisted in reporting to his superiors all misdemeanors that occurred inside his group of ten (Vega 1961: 19).

Law among the Incas was deliberately discriminatory. The higher a person's status in the hierarchy, the more law-respecting he was expected to be. As in the Aztec's system of justice, punishment was more severe for nobles than for the ordinary commoner committing the same crime. Adultery, for example, earned the commoner, or the commoner's wife, a nasty session of torture. A member of the nobility caught in adultery was condemned to death. Crime seems to have been infrequent. There was little motivation for it and punishment was certain (Karen 1975: 101-104).

A POOR EDUCATIONAL SYSTEM

Developing countries need effective education systems to provide them with manpower for public and business administration, technical posts in agriculture and industry, research and teaching. Such investment in human resources is a first priority for development. Economists long regarded education as a simple "final consumption" and manpower as a "factor of production." The experience and setbacks encountered in implementing certain development programs and plans gradually led economists to recognize that education had an essential role, not only in the success of short term programs but also in the effective achievement of long term development. It is interesting to note that the ancient civilizations of Latin America had developed educational programs more advanced than those in existence in many modern-day nations.

The Aztecs

Aztec society's concern with education was singular for its time — school was compulsory for children. They were two main types of schools, and attendance at one or the other determined social and economic status. The children of the nobility usually attended a school run by scholarly priests, in preparation for the priesthood or some high office in the state. Occasionally a talented son of a commoner gained entrance. To prepare students for future responsibilities, discipline was very strict and hours of study were long. In a vigorous intellectual regimen, young boys studied religion, astronomy, philosophy, history, poetry, rhetoric, and oratory, among other disciplines. Although the spoken language was rich and expressive and lent itself to fine subtleties, the picture writing was limited. History was passed on by oral traditions committed to memory (Meyer and Sherman 1987: 76).

Most of the other children attended one of the commoners' schools where they found a more relaxed, less intellectual atmosphere. Boys and girls were given practical instruction in basic subjects. Boys learned the rudiments of warfare, and those who excelled in the profession of arms could do very well for themselves; others had to be content with learning trades or lesser skills. Girls were instructed in the responsibilities of the household and motherhood. They were taught modesty, courtesy, and conformity (Ibid.: 76-77).

The Mayas

The Mayas' civilization was clearly the greatest to flourish in pro-Colombian America. They studied the heavens to devise precise calendars, created a true writing system and built imposing cities. However, progress in deciphering Maya writings has been slow. Their complex hieroglyphics once were thought to be incomprehensible. Not much is known about the educational system that existed within the Mayan empire.

As in almost all the early civilizations, it is extremely difficult to separate the Mayans' primitive scientific knowledge from its ritual context. The Mayas had evolved a considerable body of empirically derived information about the natural world. Arithmetic and astronomy had reached a level comparable to that achieved by the ancient Babylonians and surpassing, in some respects, that of the Egyptians. But science in the modern sense was not present. In its place there was, as with the Mesopotamian civilizations, a combination of fairly accurate astronomical data with what can only be called numerology, developed by Maya intellectuals for religious purposes (Coe 1987: 130).

Knowledge of Mayan thought represents only a tiny fraction of the whole picture. Out of thousands of books in which the full extent of their learning and ritual was recorded, only four have survived to modern times (three of them are prayer books). These are written on long strips of bark paper folded like screens and covered with gesso (Ibid.).

The Incas

The school system of the Incas seems to be similar to that of the Aztecs. The sons of the Incan nobility were educated in the imperial schools where they learned Incan history, law and religion. A body of scholars lived in Cusco, supported by the emperor and dedicated to the education of youth. These scholars were regarded with high esteem among the Incas, and their teaching duties were considered to be of the utmost importance to the welfare of the nation. The education given by these scholars was more humanistic than pragmatic, and the development of well-rounded men seems to have been of greater importance than the training of specialists. Besides history, law, and religion, students learned music, poetry, philosophy, and the art of governing. The scholars guided their students to become more urbane, skillful, and humane and taught them oratory skills.

ADMINISTRATIVE LEGACIES

The bureaucracies of the ancient civilizations seem to have faced the very same problems confronted by the bureaucracies of the developing countries. Despite the very different political framework of these ancient civilizations, their administrative practices can still guide the process of development administration in the developing countries. Economic development policies of the Aztecs, Mayas, and Incas integrated the territories of these empires in a way that has never been accomplished in Africa, Asia, and Latin America. Even post World War II Europe was geographically delineated in ways that required some careful integration policies within the new nations. The present situation in Yugoslavia is an extreme example of the problem.

In Africa, one of the major problems in the development of the continent is posed by the frontiers of the African states, a legacy of the colonial phase of their history. They were established without regard to linguistic and ethnic affiliations and often included non-related groups, some of whom did not even recognize colonial frontiers. Beyond the boundaries of practically every state are people seeking to be re-united with those within. However, as legacies of the colonial regime, they are both resented and ardently defended. These disputes can last for years, if not decades, and affect the relations between neighboring countries. Asia and Latin America had a similar experience.

When the Incas captured new provinces for example, every effort was made to continue the previous local rulers in office. But the sons of these rulers were taken as hostages to Cuzco where they received the formal upper class education. They were encouraged to marry Incan girls from the nobility before returning home in order to assure their loyalty and alliance. The Incans imposed their sun-worship religion and the Quechua language on the new subjects (Bennett 1949: 220). The spread of Quechua was vital to the process of Incan assimilation. It filtered down even to the lowest strata of society. The community of language undoubtedly created a community of minds, and Quechua played in the Incan empire a role similar to that of Latin in the Roman Emperor.

Another means of creating an organic unity among the subjects of the Incan empire was the state-planned movements of population. By imperial decree, colonies of Incas were moved to the fringes of the empire or to rebellious unassimilated regions within its boundaries. They were given lands, granted tax exemptions, honored with other privileges, and entrusted with the task of colonizing the natives and bringing them into the mainstream of Incan life. These massive movements of peoples were not exceptional, but a common policy that in a few generations altered the patterns of population settlements within the empire. These friendly assimilations helped to create a climate of unity and a common culture (Martin 1974: 12-13). The Incas had a great knowledge of the way to conquer and how to bring the new subjects into the empire by good management. The need for countries to find integration formulas to stimulate their economies and broaden their markets has become obvious over the past decades, especially in Latin America and Africa. However, the integration models have been putting more emphasis in dynamic growth of regional and national gross products than in stimulating greater social progress.

Some of the policies and practices of the ancient civilizations of the Aztecs, Incas, and Mayas reviewed in this chapter are inadequate as a model for development in modern time. The feudal social structures of these ancient civilizations belong to an archaic world. Therefore, although much can be learned from their rational administrative systems, many of their practices are unacceptable at the present. Developing countries will need to apply the same caution they use when dealing with Western models, like the Weberian one, in borrowing from these ancient civilizations the lessons that could be valuable for them.

7

A MODEL FOR PLANNING
ETHICAL TRAINING ABROAD:
THE CASE OF GUATEMALA
AND MEXICO

Chapter three suggested that one of the components of an effective administrative ethics prescription is the teaching of ethics through formal university courses and/or continuous training of public servants. Such courses and training seminars abound in the industrialized countries and several developing countries are now requesting that ethics be covered when they request technical assistance in the area of public personnel training. However, a major difficulty in planning such courses is the varying degree of cultural and other indigenous factors that might influence the effectiveness and acceptance of these foreign-conceived training seminars. This chapter suggests actual training procedures or techniques to be used in public personnel and ethical training abroad. Its focus is on the need to consider carefully the different factors that are influencing the policy-making and policy implementation process of the personnel to be trained in order to be able to develop training programs that are both adequate and relevant. The examination of these factors in the Guatemalan and Mexican bureaucracies here will illustrate the application of the methodology suggested.

Planning for ethical training include discussions on common issues in ethical behavior and public service responsibility: illustrative ethical predicaments facing public servants; feasibility of ethical education and training; building on traditional values in the design of the curricula; and optional approaches and methods for ethical education and training. Ethical training courses should also be aimed primarily at teaching cognitive skills or developing character. The character-building objective of these courses can be achieved through some appropriate instruction in applied ethics.

Training for more senior civil servants needs to be more sophisticated and should be based upon the assumptions that these officers may be assumed to have established their honesty and high motivation, that they have working experience of the temptations to act dishonestly implicit in public service, that they have supervisory and leadership roles, and that, in the course of their work, they are in contact with the political leadership. Training planed for such people should be organized around their active participation in role playing and in case studies. They should be encouraged to study and to research organizational procedures with a view to their reform as necessary to minimize opportunities for corruption, i.e., to simplify procedures, both public and bureaucratic, to remove temptation to operate inefficiently or dishonestly.

There are different levels of development between the two extremes of the underdeveloped and the developed countries. For analytical purposes, most authors situate only the category of developing ones in between. Riggs' Prismatic model is a good illustration of that (1964). However, these levels of development do not necessarily correspond to the stages of bureaucratic development attained by each one of the three groups of countries. This is quite a problem for public personnel training in these countries. The type of training which is adequate for a country is dependent on many factors that are in the periphery of the bureaucracy. To facilitate the adequate planning of training sessions, this chapter will examine ten factors that directly or indirectly influence bureaucratic performance.

The assessment process undertaken through this methodology will help determine the types of public personnel and ethical training that will allow public managers to follow suit of the policy changes and objectives. When public personnel training is not done in the framework of a broader societal context, managers cannot anticipate all the pitfalls that might oblige them to deviate from the theories learned. D.S. Lee states the consequences of such a handicap:

> When theory does not account with unanticipated contingencies, theory is rejected rather than modified to fit the circumstances. Because management theories are viewed as mutually exclusive (rather than as complementary but alternative views of reality), when theories appear to contradict each other, there is a tendency to believe that the competing theories have canceled each other out. (1990: 246)

Public personnel training can only be effective if the trainers present theories as they apply to the bureaucratic environment. The chapter will attempt to establish the types of training that would be adequate for each one of the three levels of bureaucratic development (developed, developing, and under-developed). To be able to do so, the chapter will examine each country to find out how many of the ten factors that influence bureaucratic performance are positively present. Since some of these factors can also determine the level of general economic development and modernization, it should be clear that they are being used here only to establish the level of bureaucratic development of the countries. Therefore, it is quite possible, as this analysis will show, that a country found with a very advanced bureaucratic development is traditionally considered a developing one in terms of its general economic development. Instead of using primarily the usual quantifiable economic factors, the typology is based on a broader set of societal conditions. The ten factors being used here correspond to a number of preconditions that R.W. Crawley (1965) has elaborated for determining the modernization or advancement process.

The methodology to be followed will place any country with up to three of these factors rated positively in the category of underdeveloped bureaucracies. Countries with a positive rating in four up to seven of the factors will be considered in the category of developing bureaucracies. The third group — the one of developed bureaucracies — will include any country where eight or more factors are rated positively.

The ten factors that will be reviewed in the paper will be discussed in the national context of two countries: Guatemala and Mexico. A more complete typology covering most of the African and Latin American countries can easily be constructed when applying this methodology. The data and information on the two countries are not updated because the application of the methodology requires that data collection be made immediately prior to the preparation of the training materials for the seminar. Since any data will inevitably be time-sensitive, any analysis made at a given time may easily change the results of the inquiry. The purpose of this chapter is only to illustrate how the ten factors in the methodology can be successfully applied.

CONSISTENT LAW AND ORDER

It is difficult to speak of law and order in Guatemala without expounding upon the presence of the military and its rule and influence throughout the political system. Indeed, the military is often considered to be the real government and in many instances, prevails over official government policies (Booth and Seligson 1989: 96-100). Although the country is presently ruled by a democratically elected president, the legacy of military intervention in governmental affairs still exists, resulting in violence and fear instilled in the poor indigenous masses (over 60 percent of the population is native Indian).

This has created an atmosphere of distrust and rebellion that resulted in massive counterinsurgency efforts led by the governments in power since the early 1960's, and continues even today. An article published in 1990, gives a grim account of the second democratic election in Guatemala:

> In over three decades of armed rebellion and cruel counterinsurgency, more than 100,000 people have died in Guatemala, 45,000 have disappeared, 200,000 forced into exile, and more than a million people displaced internally (Jeffrey 1991: 149).

It is said that for the government and the military, counterinsurgency has become, after twenty-five years of fighting, a type of governance and a way of life (Barry 1991: 244). However, according to a September 27, 1992 article in La Jornada, the government has begun encouraging Guatemalan refugees in Mexico to return to their country by approving the Permanent Refugee Commission's conditions for repatriation which included various civil and political freedoms, as well as the right to life and to reclaim lands.

In the past thirty years and continuing into the present, one does not see consistent patterns of law and order in Guatemala. One obvious reason is the nation's 1960-1996 civil war. During that gruesome 36-year civil war, the government used a scorched-earth campaign, raising thousand of villages and sanctioning civilian massacres. Most of the 200,000 who died were Indian peasants. Although matters appear to be moving in the right direction at the time the methodology was applied, the overall rating for this factor is negative.

In Mexico, the 1910 Revolution gave rise to a long-standing political/bureaucratic system that holds the record of the longest presidential succession in Latin America. This system has not been seriously challenged outside the established electoral system until the 1997 Mexico City mayoral election and the presidential election of July 2000. The rating for the first factor is positive in the case of Mexico.

FINANCIAL STABILITY AND THE
ABSENCE OF SEVERE INFLATION

Throughout the 1980's, Guatemala had experienced severe economic decline resulting in negative growth rates. However, the real Gross Domestic Product (GDP) in Guatemala has been increasing steadily in the first three years of the 1990's with 3.1 percent growth in 1990, 3.2 percent in 1991, 4.0 percent in 1992, and projections to hold steady at 4.0 percent in 1993 (Economist Intelligence Unit, 1992: 12). The current account deficit in 1991 was smaller than anticipated at $183 million. However, traditional exports have declined in 1992 and imports have dramatically increased causing a negative trade balance.

The net outflow through the banking system implies a loss of reserves by the monetary sector. The exchange rate for the quetzal (the monetary unity in Guatemala) has been declining in the mid 1990's; government spending has risen by 60 percent; and inflation is rising at 10 percent from earlier predictions of 7.5 percent (Ibid).

However, Guatemala has recently joined the General Agreement on Tariffs and Trade which may increase trade with Europe and will present the country in a more positive light for overall trade and financial stability. It rates positively for this factor.

The North American Free Trade Agreement (NAFTA) signed in 1992 is expected to give an unprecedented boost to the Mexican economy. Some of its provisions favored Mexican banks, and by lowering tariffs on Mexican goods, the pact will give Mexican exports an edge in the U.S. market, even though other countries in the region may produce the same products more cheaply. On economic grounds, that sort of discrimination is hard to justify. According to Levinson, in a Newsweek article of August 17, 1992, the case for the NAFTA is political, not economic. By giving Mexico an advantage, Washington hoped to cement the free-market reforms of then-President Carlos Salinas, reforms that it hoped would eventually lessen migration to the United States and reduce the risk of instability across the Rio Grande. NAFTA marks the merger of a cheap, young labor pool in Mexico with the technological, capital-intensive economies of the U.S. and Canada. This development alone — which will strongly support the free-market reforms of future Mexican administration — contributes to give Mexico a positive rating for this factor.

PROVISION OF A MINIMAL
PUBLIC SERVICE STATUTE

The present Civil Service Law of Guatemala has been in existence since 1968. It deals with the hiring, firing, hours, vacations and job classification for state workers and employees of municipalities and autonomous institutions. Few efforts have been made to change or update this law. However, in late 1986, Decree 71-86 of the Labor Code was updated to give workers, for the first time since 1954, the right to strike, unionize and collectively bargain. A new constitution, also adopted in 1986, further clarifies workers benefits and rights (Goldston 1989: 18-19).

The Civil Service Statute of Mexico guarantees the same rights. In addition, the Mexican bureaucracy has a series of agencies that provide for educational needs and public welfare. But the Mexican bureaucracy is more politicized and is one of four coalition blocs of the Partido Revolucionario Institucional, Institutional Revolutionary Party (PRI), the official government party and until July 2000, the predominant one in the country. The Mexican bureaucracy is also a vital government tool to plan and carry out the economic life of the country. But in some agencies, personal contacts are vital for employment and advancement, this resulting in poor performance. However, in other agencies, especially those involved with economic development activities, the bureaucracy seems more productive. This is a situation which is present in many countries. Usually the government is more interested on this sector of the bureaucracy, thus resulting in more trained personnel.

Both countries can be rated positively for this factor because both have a significant civil service statute.

PEACEFUL MEANS FOR RESOLVING CONFLICTS

In early 1989, Guatemalan civil servants decided to strike to demand better working conditions and improved pay and classification scales. The unrest was also due to a series of personnel layoffs the preceding month. Riot police were called in by the government to use force against the strikers. Several months later that year, the President declared a state of emergency to control the surge of public employees' strikes and price increases of basic products.

In the political arena, thousands of people have died since the late 1980's, most of them victims of terrorism from right-wing gangs. According to the human rights commissioner of Guatemala, there were 253 "extra-judicial" killings during the first half of 1992 and many of the soldiers who participated in massacres were acquitted for lack of evidence (Economist Intelligence Unit 1992: 14). Guatemalan administrations since the early 1990's have been accused of failing to enforce labor laws. There has also been much criticism concerning the inability of workers to openly form unions. Many active union members and union leaders have been "disposed of," according to a June 4, 1992 account in the Journal of Commerce. Although some progress has been made in recent years and the general picture has changed, the situation is still bleak. A human rights report released in early 2001 by the United States State Department found that witnesses, victims, prosecutors and judges have been threatened, including judges in politically charged cases who suffered gun and grenade assaults on their houses. Efforts to reform the judiciary continue, but the climate of impunity is a serious problem In addition, human rights organizations say they have credible reports of forced disappearances attributed to the police as well as reports of torture of detainees. The overall rating for factor 4 is negative for Guatemala.

In Mexico the present administration has used great skills to find ways of resolving problems arisen from public sector practices without creating open conflicts. In the past, dissidence toward the government that could not be appeased with jobs or bribes for leaders and promises for followers was then repressed. But when the pressures of dissatisfaction continued to mount, past governments would then gradually modify policies and direct the bureaucracy to meet the original demands. According to an article in La Jornada of January 10, 1992, then-President Salinas in an address to the nation called for the modernization of the state, "but not at the price of internal discord." The rating for this factor for Mexico is positive.

ORDERLY, PUBLICLY ACCEPTED MEANS
OF TRANSFER OF POWER

In the past, almost since the turn of the century, Guatemala has been run by a series of military regimes. However, in 1985, the military chose to sponsor peaceful elections of civilian candidates. These elections were said to be honest. The 1990 election and transfer of administration in 1991 were also conducted in a technically correct manner and according to Guatemalan law. Therefore, despite pre-election reports issued by Amnesty International, Americas Watch, and the Inter American Human Rights Commission stating that politically motivated murders and "disappearances" had continued at the approximate rate of 100 persons per day (Barry 1991: 140), the overall rating for Guatemala for factor 5 is positive.

As mentioned earlier, Mexico holds the record for the longest lawful presidential succession in Latin America. The Constitution of 1910 gave extraordinary powers to the president and more importantly, the absolute control over the large federal bureaucracy. In addition, when the PRI became the single political party in the country in 1929 the tradition was started for the president in power to nominate his successor. This tradition continued until 2000. The 1917 Constitution allows only one single 6-year term. The rating for Mexico for factor 5 is positive.

AN EQUITABLE TAX SYSTEM

A common problem in most under-developed and developing countries is the lack of a tax system and structure that places the burden on the rich and not on the poor. Guatemala has recently reformed its tax structures. A new emphasis has also been placed on combating the rampant problem of tax evasion. The country's tax taken as a percentage of GDP has been one of the lowest in the world (IBC International Country Risk Guide 1991). New income tax laws for the tax year of 1992 1993 determine a tax rate of 15 percent for income in the Q18,000 to Q20,000, 20 percent for those earning Q20,000 to Q65,000, and 25 percent for those earning more than Q65,000 (Economic Intelligence Unit 1992). Although poor people in Guatemala City work longer hours for less pay than the non-poor and that women earn an average of 27 percent less than men (Terrell 1989) which means that a greater burden is placed on the poorest segments of society, such inequities are not due to the tax system. Therefore, the rating for Guatemala for factor 6 is positive.

The government of Mexico raises a large portion of its revenues through income taxes, both personal and corporate. Although all citizens pay a share of their income, whoever makes more money is taxed more. The rating for Mexico for factor 6 is also positive.

AGRARIAN REFORM

Agrarian reform has been and still is a key element in the development of Guatemala. In 1952, President Arbenz proposed a badly needed agrarian reform law entitled Decree 900. The intent was to restructure land distribution in hopes of bettering the overall economic and social condition of the country (Handy 1988: 704-705). The reform effort was initially successful but later was met with great resistance from landowners. Arbenz was overthrown in 1954.

In 1986 the government tried to dissipate the concerns for land reform by making efforts to improve the pay and living conditions of the poor workers of the land. In 1987 and 1988, due to increased pressure from the Catholic church, small parcels of land were sold to peasants in hopes of pacifying the discontented masses (Goldston 1989: 32-33). In the 1990's, the government acknowledged that there is a need for land reform but its efforts to promote one have been minimal. Current figures show that less than two percent of the landowners own 65 percent of the farm land, the most highly skewed land-tenure pattern in Latin America (Barry 1991: 247). Although there is a definitive need for extensive land measures in Guatemala, there are no indications that such measures will be forthcoming. The rating for factor 7 is highly negative.

The Mexican constitution of 1917 called for drastic reforms in the government and the social life of the country. One of the reforms it mentioned was the redistribution of lands. It was not the first time that agrarian reform was being promoted nor would it be the last because most of the times little action followed these declarations of principles. Under the 1917 Constitution, agrarian holdings were limited, guaranteeing the break up of the old "hacienda" system. The constitution made it the state's constitutional obligation to distribute rural land among country people (Hoagland 1992: 38-41).

In 1992, the Salinas administration took an interesting approach to agrarian reform. When he addressed the nation in January 1992 regarding internal reforms, agrarian reforms were repeatedly mentioned. As Hoagland explains in his article:

> The 1992 Constitutional reform brings an end to distribution and should make investment in all rural land more secure. For the first time, commercial corporations will be allowed to hold and work rural land subject to some special restrictions, including a limit on size. Larger, more efficient farms should develop by allowing more freedom of action to the ejidario (communal occupation system). Control of management of the ejidos now lies with the ejidarios themselves, with minimum of state oversight. While the village land will remain inalienable, the ejido may vote to contribute its common areas to commercial corporations in exchange for stock at an approved price (Ibid.)

Thus, during the current administration, the people of Mexico are undergoing rural land reforms that will give them control of management over their land with minimal state oversight. Despite the many problems associated with this innovative program of agrarian reform, and some negative aspects it has, the overall rating for Mexico for factor 7 is positive.

DEVELOPMENT OF A HIGH DEGREE
OF CONSENSUS

The degree of consensus in Guatemala is distorted because of the disparity in the ethnic distribution of the population. Since over half of the people are Mayan Indian (Barry 1991: 262). They own very little land, are non-Spanish speakers, and are peasant farm workers. They generally feel under-represented by the elitist government which is more representative of the ladino (mixed "white") race.

An important element that is strategically interwoven into everyday events in Guatemala concerns the activity of the guerilla forces, a situation that has existed since 1962 (Ibid.: 241). In addition, the governments democratically elected do not seem to be popular with the masses. The overall turn out in these democratic elections produced a voter rate well below 50 percent. All of these conditions can hardly be considered representative of a consensus among Guatemalans. The rating for the country for factor 8 is thus negative.

As previously mentioned, former President Salinas had embarked in the early years of his administration in a campaign for modernizing his country without discord. His reform plans called for reorganization of the bureaucracy and the economy, advancement of human rights, and the establishment of clear regulations for church-state relationships. According to a La Jornada article of January 10, 1992, Salinas also promoted agrarian reforms, social reforms, modernization of education and the protection of the environment. These reforms widely welcomed by the people clearly indicate a high degree of consensus within the Mexican society. Therefore the rating for Mexico for factor 8 is positive.

PROGRESSIVE INCREASE IN THE FLOW OF DOMESTIC CAPITAL

Real GDP is progressively increasing in Guatemala, inflation has decreased since 1993 and exports are slowly increasing as are imports. These are positive signs that there is a certain confidence among the people and that domestic capital is moving. In the early 1990's figures for real GDP, consumer price inflation, merchandise exports and imports and external, confirm this progressive trend (Economic Intelligence Unit 1992). The rating for Guatemala for factor 9 is thus positive.

Mexico, after a strong performance of nearly 4 percent in economic growth in 1991, had slumped into a mild recession by the end of 1992. According to a Miami Herald article of October 17, 1992, the government pushed up interest rates on its treasury bills to 19 percent, trying to attract capital and dampen the import enthusiasm. Economic growth for 1992 was around 2.8 percent.

A good indication of Mexico's progressive increase in the flow of domestic capital are the government revenues resulting from the privatization of previously state-owned companies and services. The program, called neoliberalism, was strongly backed by the U.S. government and the International Monetary Fund and was being implemented in several other Latin

American countries. However, the Miami Herald in October 17, 1992, stated that Mexico has led the region in revenues from privatization, earning $19.8 billion from the sale of its telephone monopoly, Telefonos de Mexico, and its 18 national banks (Ibid.). The rating for the country for factor 9 is highly positive.

HONEST AND EFFECTIVE PUBLIC ADMINISTRATION

Corruption in the public sector in Guatemala is quite extensive. Embezzlement, the acceptance of gifts, and nepotism in judicial and financial offices are unethical practices readily acknowledged by many citizens. According to an October 12, 1989 article in Grafico, the extensiveness of such corruption is attributed to the number of opportunities available, as well as to the structural limitation of retribution.

President Serrano, in an April 16, 1991 interview in Prensa Libre, addressed the issue of corruption in public administration and acknowledged that it was a problem. His plans for straightening up the public sector and reforming the judicial and penal systems, also discussed in the interview, have yet to be implemented. The rating for Guatemala for factor 10 is negative.

Corruption has been traditionally a very big problem in public administration in Mexico. It was rampant in the past in almost all the levels of the bureaucracy, from the lowest civil servant to the president and his cabinet ministers. However, since taking office, former President Salinas had been combating it in many fronts. But the bureaucracy was his main target. Toward the end of 1990, the former President initiated several programs to reform the corrupt bureaucrats. One such program was designed to curb corruption among officials regulating border crossing points, airports and highways. As explained further in a newspaper article:

> The Paisano program began last year as a pilot effort to stop corruption. This year, it has been upgraded with the participation of seven government agencies. It reasons that if Mexicans know their rights, say Paisano officials, they will not be a pushover if a corrupt official uses a false pretext to try to extort money (Scott 1990).

Another example of the President's crackdown on bureaucratic corruption was the focusing of his reform program in 1991 in the Federal law enforcement agencies. He declared that the government was committed to rooting out the corruption and abuses that have long tainted Mexican law enforcement efforts.

According to a New York Times article of June 5, 1992, all federal police units were reorganized and placed under the direct strengthened control of a civilian Deputy Attorney General appointed by President Salinas. Considering these extraordinary efforts, the rating for Mexico for factor 10 is a positive one despite the fact that, after his administration several, corrupt practices of close allies and relatives have been revealed and are still being investigated in 2001.

Overall, the analysis of the ten factors influencing the behavior of public personnel in Guatemala shows that the country has a positive rating in five of these factors which according to the grading established at the beginning of the paper places Guatemala in the category of "developing" in terms of its level of bureaucratic development. It should be noted that in terms of general development Guatemala is also traditionally considered a developing country. However, in the Mexican case, all ten factors were rated positive. This places Mexico in the category of "developed" in terms of its level of bureaucratic development which is a different rating from that country's in terms of general economic development. It is traditionally viewed as an advanced developing country. The analysis has shown that in several factors one or both countries appear to be in the fringe of the necessary progress or setback to be rated positively or negatively. In the case of both countries some reforms or attempted reforms had been initiated only by administrations elected in the 1990's. Therefore, both countries should be reexamined on a regular basis to determine if their ratings have remained the same.

The type of information collected for this analysis—both the political and the economic—is quite fluid and change constantly in most developing countries. For this model to be effective, the collection of data has to be done shortly prior to the preparation of the training seminars. In addition to recent newspaper articles and information found in the Internet, a preliminary site visit could allow empirical observations that will frame the training sessions in a tightly relevant cultural, socio-political and economic context. It is obviously much easier for a country to move from one category to another in terms of its bureaucratic development than it would be in terms of its general economic development. The case of Mexico clearly establishes, at least according to the theory advanced in this chapter, that the level of bureaucratic development of a country, does not necessarily correspond to its level of economic development.

CONCLUSIONS

Although the assessment technique for determining the level of bureaucratic development of a country presented in this chapter can be used in a variety of contexts, its relevancy to public personnel and ethical training in the Third World is considerable. Trainers, both those involved in the preparation of training materials and those who actually conduct the sessions, should review the ten factors before hand to acquire a good knowledge of the ecology of the bureaucracy where the training will take place. Unfortunately, quite often trainers are retained by consulting firms because of their success in using training approaches that are widely accepted as effective. Some of these trainers might have gone to numerous countries in Latin America, Africa, Asia to duplicate their "successful" training sessions without realizing their inadequacy and irrelevance to some of these countries. There are many types of training, using many methods, but each type and each method must correspond to the level of bureaucratic development of the public personnel to be trained.

As previously stated, the purpose of this chapter is not to suggest actual training procedures and techniques to be used for public administrators. However, there should be some emphasis on the need to study carefully the societal environment of each country in order to accommodate both the internal and external changes that affect its bureaucracy. Using Guatemala and Mexico as a case study to illustrate the methodology, the chapter suggests that it is imperative that efforts for effective training of public servants, especially at the highest levels, be revisited, challenged and reformulated to meet the needs of the bureaucracy of the countries. Such revision and reformulation should be done while reviewing all the factors that determine bureaucratic performance in these countries and after addressing their level of bureaucratic development. Only then, will the training provide to public administrators the adequate skills needed to make creative policies and administer progressive programs within a realistic ethical framework.

PART IV

ETHICS AND DEVELOPMENT IN AFRICA

The two chapters of this Part deal with Africa, a continent where some countries are experiencing a deterioration of moral values, particularly public morality, the rise of corruption, financial mismanagement and financial crimes. A prominent African government official pointed out in 1994 that in African traditional values, the concept of work was acknowledged as an important value (if you are lazy, people looked down at you). But with European influence, the concept of work has taken on a different meaning because of forced labor, which had no commonality of interest. As a result, hard work is no longer valued and honored. In order to restore that value, he argued that new ethical values about the virtue of work have to be communicated to the young generations from an early age (Bigelow 1995: 20).

Many African governments are still battling entrenched bureaucracies and bloated public sectors. Other seemingly intractable problems include the lack of a strong judiciary. A great challenge will be in moving toward some kind of democratic pluralism. A prominent African official even stated that Western style democracy is destabilizing for Africa. Others say democratic freedom begets economic freedom. African leaders have been grumbling for sometime that outsiders have been thrusting alien development models on them for too long (Vasuki 1998: 35-38).

However, Africa's economic development during the decade of the 90s has been truly impressive. At last count, at least 40 of the 48 nations on the continent are participating in the International Monetary Fund (IMF)-sponsored stabilization programs, indicating that many African countries are broadly pursuing open market policies. The World Bank estimates that overall economic growth touched 4.5 percent in 1996 for the 40 countries under IMF supervision. Africa's population is projected to reach one billion by the year 2020 from the 1998 levels of around 700 million (Ibid.).

Chapter eight overviews the general status of administrative accountability in Africa. It serves as an introduction to Chapter nine, which is a case study on some of the ethical implications of foreign developmental aid to the continent. The United Nations Development Program financed an administrative reform project in the twin-islands Republic of Sao Tome and Principe between 1988 and 1994 to upgrade the administrative capability of its public service. This chapter reviews the objectives of the reform and discusses the strategy for its implementation. Such strategy comprised five tactics: a) the sensitization of the environment of the reform; b) the adaptation of an incrementalist approach; c) the creation of "reform islands"; d) the reduction of salary supplements that were being paid by the donors; and e) the privatization of some services. The chapter also examines the obstacles to reform in Sao Tome and Principe and concludes that the generalized institutional weakness of the public sector in that country will continue to hobble capacity-building efforts.

8

ADMINISTRATIVE ACCOUNTABILITY IN AFRICA

The last two decades have witnessed considerable attention to the problems of development administration, particularly administrative accountability. This is because of the increasing involvement of the state with the development process in the developing world, and of the growing participation of various groups and organizations in the socio-economic and political development in the industrialized nations. For the purpose of this chapter, administrative accountability (i.e., accountability by public administrators or bureaucrats) and political accountability (i.e., accountability by the political leadership or the decision-making body) are discussed under the same umbrella as administrative accountability. The reason for this is because in most countries in the developing world, there really is no sharp demarcation between the two. Politicians not only make the decisions at the top, but they at the same time act as administrators in carrying out governmental decisions to promote development.

Although accountability is not a new concept, it was not until recent years that its application has gained a world-wide popularity. The Holy Bible, one of the oldest documents in the history of mankind, eloquently "tells us that we are accountable for our stewardship on earth" (Sabine 1973: 3). The concept is further expressed in a similar fashion in Saint Luke: "And he called him, and said unto him, How is it that I hear this of thee? give an account of thy stewardship; for thou mayest be no longer steward" (Luke 16: 2).

It is abundantly clear that the connotation of accountability as used in The Bible, is not entirely different from our understanding of the term in contemporary socio-economic and political life, particularly in bureaucratic behavior. The Bible stresses individual accountability only to God, whereas in modern usage, governments and elected officials are generally held answerable to the people who elected them to office.

The point of interest here is that either connotation clearly indicates that one set of variables, "A" (individuals or leaders) is accountable to another set of variables, "B" (God, or the people). In the Biblical sense, accountability is based on individual stewardship to God, whereas elected officials (singularly and/or collectively) are answerable to the people they represent. God created men and women and bestowed upon them the precious things in life, for which they are accountable to Him. Similarly, citizens of any country, or any group of people belonging to an organization, etc., can and do elect their leaders who then become answerable to the people for the former's actions. Even in situations where such leaders have assumed office illicitly, the tendency that the people nevertheless expect them to be accountable cannot be overlooked. The rampant demonstrations and riots that take place under authoritarian regimes are manifestations of this phenomenon.

When governments are formed or individuals are elected to offices, they invariably are endowed with objectives, resources, powers, "respect," and above all, responsibility (Elliot and Ali 1984; Rosen 1982; Ghartey 1987). Regrettably, increasing evidence from around the world shows that many leaders (elected and non-elected alike), once they assume office, do not honor the promises they make to the people. On the contrary, they sidetrack and become corrupt, avaricious, inefficient, and incapable of fulfilling the anticipation of the people.

The plethora of cases of corruption, mismanagement, and misappropriation of public funds in many industrialized nations in recent years bear testimony to this claim. From the Nixon Watergate scandal of the 1970s, to various corruptive practices in the City of Miami discussed in chapter three (all in the United States), the Honecker misconduct in the former East Germany, and the Geisha corruption cases in Japan are just a few examples of why accountability has become a serious problem in the industrialized countries. These examples suggest that accountability is a problem not only in the developing world but in fact, a world-wide one. It is rather its nature and degree that make the difference. The democratic system of checks and balances serves to minimize domination and control, which tend to lead to corruption and misappropriation of public funds.

It has already been indicated that it is the nature and scope of accountability that essentially determine socio-economic and political development. For instance, "Inadequate accountability forms the thresholds of political instability, and social and political strife. Inadequate accountability leads, among other things, to waste, depletion of resources without compensation, erosion of public confidence, sluggish economic growth, and sustained poverty, misery and underdevelopment" (Ghartey 1986: 138).

Today, the term "accountability" has become a popular word in every corner of the world. From Lagos to Tokyo, and from Cape Town to Washington D.C.; in every city or town anywhere, leaders are more than ever before being held accountable for their actions or inactions. What has prompted this upsurge of concern with accountability the world over? Is accountability a universal phenomenon? How does the concept relate with African development?

ADMINISTRATIVE ACCOUNTABILITY

There is no single or precise definition of the word "accountability." As Gephart explains, "accountability has been everyone's watchword, but its meaning is clouded and elusive. Concurrently, related methodology and techniques are either unclear or totally unknown to those intimately involved. As many states have demonstrated, "it is easier to legislate than to accomplish" (Ghartey 1987: 86). In spite of the complexities of the term, there seems to be sufficient similarity between definitions and concepts to warrant a general frame of reference, that elected officials must be held answerable to the people they represent (Elliot and Ali 1984; Rosen 1982; Stogdill 1981).

Accountability implies the responsibility by elected officials to provide an account of their actions or performance to the people. It means an evaluation or assessment of leadership performance and conduct. Accountability implies that the people must be given the opportunity to pass judgment on their appointed or elected officials (Elliot and Ali 1984). In the absence of such a system, glaring criminal misconduct becomes menacing and interminable.

Accountability is also associated with recording and summarizing business and financial transactions in books and analyzing, verifying, and reporting the results" (Webster's New Collegiate Dictionary 1973: 8) to the public or members of particular organization. "The extension and application of accounting concepts and techniques beyond the enterprise framework to both qualitative and quantitative economic, social and political activities has not received much public attention. Such broader involvement of accounting in the social, political and economic spheres is referred to as accountability" (Ghartey 1987: 6). According to B.L.R. Smith, "Accountability is to be understood in the broadest sense as deriving from the multiple checks and points to access into the political system. There must be many guardians at different points any of which can command attention and cause review of administrative accountability" (Ghartey 1987: 47). It is worthy of note that, "In more modern times, we see accountability well defined in business and industry. A supermarket is accountable for the produce it sells — if it is spoiled, the consumer may bring it back for a refund. A corporation is accountable for its earnings record — if the record is poor, the shareholders may replace the manager" (Sabine 1973: 4).

It is crystal clear that the concept of accountability implies that elected and appointed officials (in government and private organizations) are responsible to the people they represent. In this sense, an obvious distinction can be ascertained here that accountability is one of the characteristics of constitutional democracy, while it is presumably absent within the principles of totalitarianism. Implicit in accountability is that elected officials ranging from district officers to Heads of State are both legally and politically answerable for their actions (Plano and Greenberg 1982).

It is abundantly clear thus far, that accountability encompasses all aspect of human relations — in politics, education, business, and so forth. For example, Edward Wynne defines accountability as the "system or arrangements that supply the public, as well as schoolmen with accurate information about school output performance" (Sabine 1973: 144). In the same vein, it "means the continuing assessment of the educational achievement of pupils in a school system, the relations of levels attained to the state and community and to the citizens and taxpayers of the community" (Sabine 1973: 3). Ghartey points out that, "Accountability could take several forms including disclosure of: efficiency and effectiveness of government and political bodies; the economic activities of an entire nations; social contribution of business to society; and the involvement of accountants in the measurement of national wealth and social accounting generally" (Ghartey 1987: 35).

Thus, accountability is essentially a continuous process involving an explanation for, or an assessment of the actions and performance of those having preservation of public money, public property, and human and natural resources (Stogdill 1981; Ghartey 1987). This implies that leaders charged with national resources are responsible for the judicious and effective mobilization and utilization of the resources. Given the plausibility of this hypothesis, one would perhaps ask why then, in spite of the fact that every nation is endowed with some amount of resources, countries in the North have "developed" while those in the South remain "undeveloped"? A general discussion of accountability in the African context will help answer this question.

ACCOUNTABILITY IN AFRICA

Perhaps only a few countries in recent history have suffered from socio-economic and political turmoil on the scale comparable to that of many countries in Africa. While a complex set of reasons account for the African predicament, one critical explanatory factor is the problem of administrative accountability.

Implicit in the concept of accountability is that leaders are not only answerable for their actions but also they are responsible, to a large extent, for the material well-being of the citizens. However, in many African countries as in other parts of the developing world, despotic and repressive regimes make the attainment of these things virtually impossible. The ever-increasing control of governments of the national economy, and the centralization of powers and resources deprive the masses the chance to become active participants in national development (Bryant and White 1982 and 1984; Hansen and McMillan, eds. 1986).

As already indicated, accountability has become a popular word among countries the world over. Evidence shows that this is mainly because of the increasing occurrences of decay in the state machinery (the problems of autocratic regimes, massive corruption, waste, mismanagement, etc.), and the overall disappointing record of development.

The authoritarian rule in most African countries, and the increasing involvement of the state with natural resources and in the lives of private citizens provoke a limitation of people's freedom, and of justice and basic human rights. Through the practice of oppressive rule in many African countries, therefore, accountability seems to have lost its practical meaning. To quote Ghartey, "The main root of power struggle, underdevelopment and misery in Africa has been attributed to inadequate accountability manifesting itself chiefly in corruption and economic mismanagement. The power that permeates the public bureaucracy grows out of the almost absolute discretion African leaders and public officers generally exercise and the inadequate of the present controls in the bureaucracy" (Ghartey 1986: 89). In describing the horrors in human suffering in the developing countries, he mentions that, "As a result of autarchy, oppression, repression, inadequate accountability, and economic mismanagement, the majority of innocent citizens remained cut off from the benefits of economic growth in the developing countries between 1960 and 1973" (Ibid: 90).

Other observers attribute the socio-economic and political upheaval in Africa to inadequate accountability (Lawrence, ed. 1986; World Bank 1984). The use of the phrase "inadequate accountability" is considered more appropriate for this analysis in the sense that it implies that accountability is not totally lacking in Africa. As indicated earlier, no society is entirely devoid of some form of accountability in its administrative machinery. It can be argued that even under autocratic regimes, there is some level of accountability. It is important to point out that accountability is not totally lacking in Africa. For instance, according to Ruth First, in the Upper Volta (now Burkina Faso), President Maurice Yameogo went to trial, charged with embezzling money while in office (First 1970: 103). She also wrote that, "In Ghana, patronage was more rigorously controlled, for there was a national policy for the development of state enterprise and for the curbing of the private business sector; but the group intent on accumulating property while praising the constraints imposed by the state, often managed to elude them: (Ibid.: 103). To illustrate this point further, the creation of the Citizens' Vetting committee in Ghana in 1981, was to check corruption, embezzlement, and so on (Magubane and Nzongola-Ntalaja 1983). The concept and practice of accountability in some traditional African societies was unparalleled. As an example, "In tribal practice, the power of a chief was balanced by the requirements of consultation in which every member of the tribe has an opportunity to participate" (Dodge 1966: 29). As pointed out in chapter three, many African countries elaborate anti-corruption laws in the books. Four African public administration scholars were cited and all agreed that despite existing mechanisms of control, their countries' public accountability systems could still improve significantly. So accountability has a long history in African tradition, although the abuse of power, corruption, and misappropriation of public funds have rendered Africa the focus of international scrutiny of the problem of administrative accountability.

In analyzing accountability vis-a-vis African development, it is important to emphasize "participation." As pointed out earlier, repressive governments deny the citizens an opportunity to fully participate in the development process. Without the realization and utilization of citizens' productive potentials and creative energies, no country can develop. This implies that in order for many African countries to improve their development record, leaders must be accountable in the sense of respecting human rights and permitting the people to use their own talents and energies to better their lives. The heart of the matter is that no country has ever been developed by another (Uchendu 1976), and that only the African people can develop themselves, As Stone and Stone (1976) aptly put it, "The priceless asset of a country is its human resource. Great emphasis must therefore be placed on a society's perception of human life, to man's intellectual and spiritual potential" (Barratt el al., 1976: 196). The implication of all this is to suggest that in order for African countries to achieve sustained development, governments must be accountable for their actions, including permitting citizens to participate in the development process. And by participation, we mean involvement in the decision-making through project implementation and evaluation. Implicit in the usefulness of accountability is the fact that, "Human beings seem to function better and be more productive when treated as though they can make useful contributions to decisions that affect them, regardless of the setting" (Lassey and Fernandez 1976: 1). For example, if leaders permitted popular and more active participation, people would be more involved and development would occur.

The point of all this is to suggest that when accountability becomes a problem at the top, it also originates an impasse at the bottom, and the pattern repeats itself unless drastic measures are taken to resolve the problem. It is important to point out that since not all African countries suffer from authoritarian rule, some governments have assuredly performed better in the area of accountability. Observers agree that the relatively impressive economic performance in the Ivory Coast, Kenya, Tanzania, and Zambia, among others, can be attributed largely to political stability, which is a reflection of effective administrative accountability. The most conspicuous difference between despotic regimes and democratic governments is that under oppressive regimes, leaders are accountable only to themselves, whereas constitutional democracy guarantees the citizens the opportunity to hold elected officials accountable. To illustrate, "Incompetence, dishonesty, indifference, and arrogance in agencies of government make good copy, and therein lies the news media's basic power for holding government bureaucracies accountable" (Rosen 1982: 27). It is for these reasons that the development riddle in Africa has often been attributed to inadequate accountability, albeit inadequate accountability is only a significant part of the problem.

CONCLUSIONS

As said before, administrative accountability refers to the liability of public servants to give a satisfactory account of the use of official power or discretionary authority to the people. In democracies, various formal and objective methods and procedures have been gradually evolving to ensure the bureaucrat's accountability and responsiveness to the public will. However, in developing countries where the bureaucracy is the chief agent of social and economic change and progress, bureaucrats have a wide range of discretionary authority to perform their functions. No clear norms and precedents exist to guide system of public control over the bureaucracy. Different factors complicate further this task. Some of these factors are: political (totalitarian regimes, like the military, that rely heavily on technocrats to keep the machinery of the state running, thus decreasing pressure from the top for administrative accountability); economic (low pay and lack of alternative economic opportunities that encourage corruptive practices); cultural (an authoritarian administrative culture that stimulates arbitrary use of power) etc.

Some methods and strategies are actually being experimented in some developing countries (often under the guidance and pressures of international donors) to increase bureaucratic accountability.

This chapter has attempted to explain the interplay of administrative accountability and development in Africa, and several conclusions have been reached in the process: First, it has become obvious that accountability is in fact not a new concept, as its frequent use in recent years tend to suggest.

Second, it has also been noted that while the term has not gained a universal definition, its basic tenets are nevertheless embedded in the socio-economic and political systems of all societies, democratic and non-democratic alike. Some societies have survived partly because through accountability, human beings have been able to avoid total self-destruction.

Third, it is clear that today, massive corruption, fraud, and mismanagement have become a major problem in many societies. It is quite indicative that the nature and scope of accountability may differ in African countries that are authoritarian, although the current socio-economic and political uprising all over the world also suggests that lack of accountability is a universal problem.

9

THE PROBLEMS WITH ADMINISTRATIVE REFORM IN A MINISTATE: THE CASE OF SAO TOME AND PRINCIPE

The two volcanic islands, with a population of only 128,000, are a legacy of the Portuguese empire and achieved independence only in 1975. When independence was declared there was a mass exodus of the 4,000 or so Portuguese settlers who feared reprisals just as they did in their other African colonies. That exodus left the country with virtually no skilled labor, a 90 percent illiteracy rate, one African doctor and many abandoned cocoa plantations. Unlike in Portugal's other African colonies, independence in Sao Tome and Principe gave birth to a moderate government, but events soon forced it to take a sharp turn to the left. In the early 1980's the country looked increasingly towards the communist world and 75 percent of the islands skilled labor was provided by Cuba. Much of the remaining labor force, in the form of teachers, technicians and agricultural experts, was provided by Portugal.

Between 1988 and 1990, the United Nations Development Program (UNDP) financed an administrative reform project in Sao Tome and Principe (STP). This first project established a data bank and organized some training seminars but the absence of clear political directives prevented it from having a pragmatic strategy for a reform of the entire public sector. In September 1990, a new constitution was adopted allowing for multi-parity participation in the political process. Subsequently, national elections were held in early 1991, which brought the opposition to power. Under some guidance from the World Bank, the new government realized that successful policy formulation and implementation would require a significant improvement in administrative and institutional capacity in the two-islands country. Technical assistance was requested from UNDP to finance a new administrative reform program.

In the summer of 1992 a team of three experts went to STP and formulated a project (STP/92/504) that would disburse $450,000 over a two-year period. Consistent with the objective of reducing the Government's direct role in the economy, public enterprises were to be encouraged and key governmental units strengthened. The project itself was quite limited but its seed money was supposed to attract contributions from other donors. Considerable resources were needed to improve economic and financial management, including customs administration. Institutional capacity building would also require the streamlining and strengthening of the civil service. Available data indicate that there are about 4,000 civil servants, one for every 32 Santomeans. This ratio might be the highest or one of the highest in the world. In the industrialized democracies the number of public servants in relation to population ranges from 4.4 per cent in Japan to 16.3 per cent in Sweden. In a recent study, the average ratio was about 10 per cent in the developed democracies, whereas in a selection of developing countries it was only around 4 per cent. In 1981, the number of bureaucrats in the United States represented 7.78 per cent of the population. That percentage included both the central government (1.87 per cent) and state and local government (5.91 per cent). By adding those working in non-financial enterprises (0.29 per cent) the total U.S. public sector represented only 8.07 per cent of the population (Rowat 1988: 441-44). The project formulated an action plan directed at restructuring the various ministries, and retaining personnel with the objective of increasing productivity and efficiency. The author of this book was the Mission Chief of a United Nations team that visited Sao Tome and Principe in the summer of 1992 to formulate the administrative reform project. He returned there in the Spring and the Summer of 1993 as the non-resident Chief Technical Advisor of the project.

By the end of the project, it was expected that about 15 percent of total government employees would retire or be retrenched. The social security law had been recently modified to encourage early retirement; other retrenched employees were to benefit from several pay arrangements. The reduction of the civil service supposedly would free up budgetary resources to allow an increase in the remuneration of remaining employees, based on qualifications and performance criteria.

The administrative reform project's study was conducted to determine the exact situation of the civil service of the country. The ensuring diagnostics gave the government the elements needed to establish the norms of the service (number of employees, qualifications; positions classification, salaries, resources, training needs, and the development of human resources). It also gave to the government the capacity to define the strategy of the reform proper and to manage its application.

THE SOCIO-ECONOMICS SETTING

There exits no systematic reliable data to facilitate analysis of the Socio-political problems of STP in terms of its possible participation in a larger, more diversified, economy. The World Development 1993, the sixteenth in this annual series published by the World Bank, includes the world development indicators, which offer selected social and economic statistics on 127 countries but exclude STP. A similar publication by The World Resources Institute did not mention STP either in its most recent annual publication. However UNDP in its Human Development Report 1993 gathered enough data on 173 countries, including STP, to establish a scale of Human Development Index. (HDI), discussed previously in chapter two. It found that fifty five countries had high human development in 1993, fifty six had medium human development, and the remaining sixty two had low human development. Sao Tome and Principe was ranked No. 125 and fell in the low human development category. The following data were used by UNDP to arrive at that conclusion:

Life expectancy at birth (years) 65.500
Adult literacy rate (%) 63.000
Mean years of schooling 2.300
Literacy index 0.550
Schooling index 0.180
Education attainment 1.290
Real GDP per capita (ppp$) 6.000
Adjusted real GDP per capita 6.000
Adjusted development index 0.374
GNP per capita rank minus HDI rank 12.000

(UNDP 1993: 136)

The UNDP report ranked STP No. 1 in official development assistance received per capita: U.S. $480, way above every other countries of the Third World. The next country with the highest per capita technical assistance aid is another former Portuguese colony, Cape Verde at U.S. $268. Only five other countries received an amount above U.S. $200 per capita. Although in absolute terms the amount of assistance, U.S. $48 millions, is not extraordinary, in the context of a country with a total population of 128,000 people it is excessively high (UNDP Alternatives, Inc. 1993: 172-73).

Economic scarcity in Sao Tome is further complicated by the fact that the national currency is very weak. Hard currency of any form commands a higher black market exchange rate. Although the black market is illegal, it is openly tolerated. Since most of the competent civil servants work in some projects, their dollar salaries make their wages up to 50 times higher than their previous national salaries. This imbalance makes it almost impossible for them to return to the civil service. They are constantly looking for positions in donors-financed projects. In addition, those who are not involved in projects spend considerable amount of time trying to get into one. This permanent race for positions outside the civil service exists at every level (from chauffeurs, secretaries, to high level administrators) and makes any attempts at administrative reform appeared ludicrous.

Since the early 1990's, the government of STP has been implementing a growth-oriented structural adjustment program supported by the World Bank and the International Monetary Fund. As in other African countries, this program was a response to the following two major challenges facing Africa in the last decade of the 20th century: a) to reverse the trend of economic decline which has beset the region since the 1970's and; b) to strengthen the capacity of the economies to participate as important and effective partners in the global economy in the next century. These structural adjustment programs policies have had two main components. The first involved stabilization of the economy through measures to reduce or remove external and internal imbalances. This called for managed reductions in expenditures to bring about an orderly adjustment of domestic demand to the reduced level of external resources available to the country. The second component involved measures to achieve structural changes that will contribute to economic recovery and long-term growth. This required changes in relative prices; and institutional reforms, designed to make the economy more efficient, more flexible and better able to use resources in a way that will generate long-term growth. These changes were expected to improve resource allocation and increase the resilience of the economies to future shocks (African Development Bank 1993: 152). But the structural adjustment programs have been pursued mainly as independent national programs. On the whole, this initiative has yielded only limited results in STP, and only a handful of African countries can claim significant achievement so far. The government of STP viewed the administrative reform program as an essential element for building the public sector capability for implementing the structural adjustment program. The structural adjustment Program in STP emphasized the following policies and reforms for 1992-1994:

• The rehabilitation of the cocoa sector, diversification of agriculture, and development of the fishing, forestry, and tourism sectors;

- The promotion of the role of the private sector in the economy, primarily through further liberalization of the exchange, trade and pricing regimes; land reform; parastatal restructuring; and clarification of investment incentives;
- The execution of the public investment program, focused primarily on the development of the social sectors of education and health, and on energy, infrastructure, and agriculture; and financed only on highly concessional terms; and
- The implementation of a tax reform and restructuring of the financial system, as well as a tightening of fiscal and monetary policies.

The present emphasis on structural and institutional reforms has not always been the focus of IMF programs. When it was founded in 1945, its main purpose was to help operate a system of fixed exchange rates, in which all currencies were pegged to the dollar, in turn fixed with respect to gold, that experts then considered necessary to encourage international trade. That system was successful. Differences in inflation between countries forced many to alter their currency values. When the fixed-rate system collapsed completely in 1971, the IMF turned into a new approach to reach their original objective. It is very puzzling to observe the present emphasis placed on structural adjustments in Africa by the World Bank while a very recent study by the bank clearly states that incomes in some African nations have declined nearly 20 per cent since 1977 despite improvements in economic policies. The World Bank is the World's biggest source of aid loans, committing about 25 billion a year. Together with its sister organization, the International Monetary Fund, it is capable of putting massive pressure on the African nations to receive loans in exchange for agreements to improve their economies. A World Bank study of 29 African nations that have made major economic policy changes in recent years found that while a few have taken positive steps to hold down taxes, inflation and budget deficits, it generally hasn't meant higher income for the World's poorest continent. For every $100 that Africans earned in 1977 they made about $82 in 1992. The bank calculated that in Mozambique, the war-ravaged former Portuguese colony, the average income of its 16 million people fell to $60 each in 1992 from $80 the year before. In the United States, the average was $23,120. The chief economist of the World Bank concedes that the sort of structural adjustments the bank is advocating is "emotionally charged" in Africa. According to a Miami Herald. article of March 13, 1994, many African economic elites believe that they are simply not in a position to compete on the world market in most areas and that pulling down import barriers and forcing them to go head-to-head with countries like South Korea or Argentina would devastate many of their home-grown industries .

THE OBJECTIVES OF THE
REFORM PROJECT

The second administrative reform project financed by UNDP in Sao Tome and Principe (STP/92/504) had three broad objectives. The first one was the elaboration of a global plan and strategy for administrative reform that would include:

a. A functional analysis of the public sector in order to rationalize structures and organization in the context of existing human resources;
b. A new statute of the public sector in the framework of the new organizational model to be developed for the Santomean public administration;
c. A plan for salary motivation based on the existence of internal and external financial resources available;
d. An information system as a means of support for an improved management of the personnel strategy and the public function; and
e. The reinforcement of the institutional and analytic capacity of the National Center for Administrative Reform. The staffing of the National Center for Administrative Reform (CENRA) was revamped at the initiation of the project. Since its staff was to receive salary supplements from the project, the government fired the experienced director who had negotiated the project and replaced him with a protege of the Prime Minister who was his chief of staff. The new director had a degree in chemistry and no experience whatsoever with administrative reform works. In protest, the United Nations withheld payment of his salary for more than six months but finally worked out a compromise since the government was intransigent on this matter.

The second objective was the elaboration of a human resources development and training strategy based on the new statute of the public sector.

The Third objective was the creation of an interministerial committee to coordinate external technical assistance. This third objective was included in the project solely to allow UNDP to use some project funds to hire one secretary and buy a computer and some office equipment to facilitate the task of the office of the Prime Minister in the coordinating of external technical assistance. There was never any intention nor attempt to create a new institution to carry that office's function.

During the first year of the 2-year project, STP/92/504 was being implemented with the assistance of a non-resident Chief Technical Advisor (CTA). The CTA visited the project twice a year to review progress and plan the next stages of implementation. While he was out of STP, a national project director and four national experts carried on. They were assisted by two United Nations volunteers. Some Short-term international experts also worked on the project to provide assistance in specific phases of its development. The non-resident CTA model is a very good one in theory. In addition to the savings involved, a non-resident CTA can continuously bring a fresher perspective to the project. This is particularly true in places, like Sao Tome and Principe, that are fairly isolated.

In addition to several training activities, financed with funds from the Swedish government, the project revised the organic law of each ministry and revised their organizational charts to match each existing positions with the function of the ministries described in the organic laws. This process would allow each minister to find out how many people are really needed for conducting the business of the ministry.

All employees were divided into three groups: a) the ones that were needed for the operation of the ministry and were capable of fulfilling their function; b) those needed but who required some training (the project would then target them for the training courses it was conducting) and; c) those who should leave the civil service. The project itself did not have the resources needed to relocate the individuals of the third group into other sectors of employment. Because of the scarcity of these sectors, the government of STP was hoping that additional funds would be made available by donor countries and the international institutions to help in the creation of such sectors.

Project Strategy

Often the strategy for an administrative reform program is much more important than the objectives of the reform, because it places the emphasis on organizational changes. As in the case of economic plans, it should be formulated without necessarily thinking about its eventual implementation. Such implementation will not only be the execution of decisions already made but a series of incremental decisions and actions that will redefine the original decisions. One of the biggest problems of administrative reform implementation is to look at these decisions as mere actions execution. A good strategy has to help discover the effective means for influencing and positively changing the system itself.

Administrative reform programs involve planned and durable actions that will eventually change the behavior of the civil servants. One of the conditions for a viable reform is often the existence of internal and/or external pressures. In the case of STP there was little internal pressure. But the external ones, primarily from the World Bank and the International Monetary Fund, were enormous. These organizations correctly diagnosed that salary payments absorbed most of the country's revenues and that despite the presence of a large number of civil servants, or perhaps because of this overstaffing, the Santomean administration was inefficient and incapable of implementing the economic and fiscal policies necessary for the development of the country. On the other hand the prospects for success in administrative reform would be greater if it were distanced from externally imposed conditionalities (UNDP 1993: 232).

The strategy designed for STP/92/504 comprised five tactics:

a.   Sensitize the environment of the reform.
b.   Adapt an incrementalist approach
c.   Create "reform islands"
d.   Reduce the salary supplements being paid by the donors
e.   Privatize some services.

Sensitize the environment of the reform: Although an administrative reform program is normally designed to create changes in the civil service, it is important that those changes be fully understood and accepted not only by the bureaucrats, but also by the other sectors of the community that have ties with the bureaucracy. This was one of the first tactic used. In July 1992, during the mission to formulate the project, the mission Chief gave a public lecture to discuss the reform. A year later, in July 1993, in his new capacity of non-resident Chief Technical Advisor of the project he delivered another public lecture to discuss the strategy of the reform. Other activities were also conducted to sensitize those high ranking civil servants who were still resistant to the ideas of the project.

Adapt an incrementalist approach: The experience of administrative reforms in other countries suggests that a reform strategy should preferably adapt an incrementalist approach where the different phases start gradually. This conclusion is also true for other institutional reforms in general. Empirical observation suggests that a speedy reform of institutional systems is not feasible. A more realistic approach is to desegregate, identify the dimensions of the management problems that create the most severe obstacles to the attainment of the objectives of development. To reach a decision on the right priorities to be established, the following questions were addressed:

- What are the problems whose solutions will have the greatest impact on the application of the reform program?
- What is the proper order in which to address these problems?
- Should the solution of a particular problem follows the one of another problem?
- What are the easiest problems to solve?

The strategy was to always address first the problems that were the easiest to solve. This strategy was also adopted in the selection of the government ministries where the reforms would be first introduced. Ministries who were known to be resistant to the project were not approached in the initial stage. The ministries that were sympathetic were chosen for the first activities. This was done to diminish the risks of failure and help gather a momentum for the project.

Create "reform islands": Although the reform program would eventually target the entire civil service, the strategy of the project was to place a priority for reform on the ministries that were vital for the application of the economic development plans of the government of STP. The Ministry of Finance was the first one chosen since its good operation would have a favorable impact on the rest of the civil service.

Reduce the salary supplements being paid by the donor: The project recognized that the best solution would be a rapid and comprehensive administrative reform that would provide adequate salaries to the public bureaucrats. This would eliminate the need for salary supplements. Unfortunately the economic situation of STP did not permit such a solution.

The existing system allowed each donor to pay supplements to the civil servants who work in externally-financed projects. Such salary supplements were justified, according to some donors, because of the increased tasks and responsibilities imposed by the projects. But because of the large number of projects being carried out in the country, almost all capable bureaucrats worked in one of them. Their salaries from these projects were paid in foreign currency, a situation that allowed them to either obtain maximum exchange rates at the black market or to buy in hard currency shops that sell imported goods and that are usually patronized by foreigners. The disparity in salary between them and the rest of the bureaucracy was such that they could never fully reintegrate in their former positions. As soon as a project's financing ends, those who work in it run to new projects, even in sectors quite different from their previous ones. Such a situation made it almost impossible to secure the sustainability of the Santomean institutions. Two American scholars, Brinkernoff and Goldsmith, in trying to answer the question: "What are sustainable institutions?," argued that in a strict sense the term is redundant since institutions are, by definition, sustained ways that people interact. They stated that in development circles the conventional meaning of the expression refers to consciously designed organizations which according to Honadle and Vansant (1985) do one of the following: 1) they survive over time as identifiable units, 2) they recover some or even all of their costs, and 3) they supply a continuing stream of benefits. None of these three criteria taken alone, recognize Brinkerhoff and Goldsmith, is a satisfactory way of defining sustainability. They view a sustainable institution as one that has earned the veneration of a sufficient body of people so that it gets the continuing encouragement and support it needs to handle, at a minimum, a stable volume of transactions (Brinkerhoff and Goldsmith 1991: 1-2).

A 1995 UNDP mission to STP had suggested the creation of an extra-budgetary facility that would centralize all payments of salary supplements to government employees. This fund would then be used to increase the salaries of civil servants who are still in the administration and play a vital role in the application of the government economic plans. This plan was patterned on a Bolivian Model. The donor community in that country financed a $6-million foundation to pay the salaries of 500 high-level government posts. This financing was extra budgetary and not subject to IMF ceilings on the wage bill. This kind of arrangement was consistent with ideas being put forward for possible solutions to the salary supplements problem in African countries (UNDP 1993: 228).

Privatize some services: The basic idea was to encourage individuals and institutions from the private sector or non-profit organizations to carry on some of the activities that were actually being conducted by the government. The objective of the reform was to strengthen the capacity of the government. But this capacity could also exist in the private sector. There are several governmental activities that can be performed more efficiently by the private sector. The strategy of the project was to identify these activities and to reorient its technical assistance towards the creation of institutions, organizations and cooperatives that would operate under the direction of individuals or groups outside the government. These cooperatives would have a better chance to keep functioning at the end of the technical assistance than the activities financed inside the public sector.

The privatization of some activities in each ministries would help in reorganizing the ministries. They would keep only their basic functions and would delegate other activities to entities in the private sector. In some cases, group of civil servants could be encouraged to form private companies or cooperatives to accomplish these tasks, with some initial financial aid from donors. The cooperatives for example could be financed by funds from the African Development Bank that are already affected to a social adjustment project in STP and funds from UNDP affected to STP for community initiatives. The activities of the reform had to create job opportunities outside the civil service to allow the government to reduce the number of public servants without creating a disastrous political and economic situation in the country.

OBSTACLES TO REFORM IN STP

Some of the serious administrative problems confronting Sao Tome are the same as those that exist in many other countries that are attempting administrative reforms:

- Low rationality content in policy making;
- The prevalence of too many small competitive units;
- Lack of preparation of the bureaucrats;
- Disorganized financing;
- Inadequacy of safeguards against abuse of discretionary power;
- Unevenness of performance (Caiden 1970: 81).

Relationships among executives in the Sao Tome government suffered in many cases from faulty communication. In many instances bureaucratic interactions were characterized by various forms of defensive behavior. An American scholar observed this type of situation in a Latin American country and stated that this form of behavior bears much similarity to that described by Victor A Thompson as "bureaupathic." Thompson uses the term to portray the rigid and ritualistic performance of role as means to escape from insecurity. In this situation, the bureaupathic official would stress the rights of office rather than abilities (Hopkins 1967: 110). Bureaupathology is often found in countries that are going through the process of administrative reform.

In addition to the engrained insecurity and incompetence of a majority of the Santomean civil servants, the political climate in the country was not appropriate for real reforms to take place. In a citation that fits quite well the Santomean situation, Geddes (1991: 373) quoted Hirshman to point out that administrative reforms in Latin America have constantly been opposed by those who have found in bureaucratic jobs a "refuge from which to make a last-ditch stand for their right to a quiet, incompetent existence" (Hirschman 1958: 154). National elections were scheduled for early 1995 and some early campaigning has started. Asking the government to reduce the number of civil servants at that time would considerably reduce its ability to retain power. Thus even if the government was totally committed to the reform, it probably would be under pressure to delay it. Why should leaders absorb the costs of reform while their successors stand to reap the benefits in a strengthened bureaucracy?

Simultaneous political and administrative responsibilities cause additional tensions and diminished the priority of the reform, as many high ranking civil servants get involved in the campaign. But the campaign was only increasing a political situation that was already affecting the bureaucracy. Often, mid-level civil servants had considerable influence with the governing party apparatus and/or the prime minister himself. This is bound to happen in a society as compact as the one of STP. For example, when the Minister of Finance was presented with the list of positions that should be eliminated in his ministry, he could not act on it. Several of the bureaucrats who were about to loose their positions mobilized considerable support from outside political forces and obliged the minister to delay any action.

An American scholar who studied administrative reform in seven Arab states concluded that many common obstacles to administrative reform come from within the bureaucracy itself (Jreisat 1988: 94). This is something that definitely applied to Sao Tome and Principe, even at the highest level of its civil service. The attempts at reforms were insincere efforts to introduce changes aimed at satisfying the demands of foreign aid donors especially the World Bank and the International Monetary Fund. The emphasis was on doing as little as possible while appearing to do much more.

Another problem is the fact that reform and all administrative change policies are designed by technical experts, but depend for their implementation on administrators and politicians (Hammergreen 1983: 15). As pointed out in chapter five of this book, successful implementation of reform polices in developed societies has depended on two important features of the Western bureaucracies: their decentralized structure and their adherence to a set of characteristics patterned after Max Weber's bureaucratic model. Both of these features are lacking in the Santomean bureaucracy. Even if these features were present they could not have surmounted the limitations of cultural transference. The project experts were under pressure to apply ideas, techniques, and procedures which have worked in the more developed nations but which are not appropriate in a less Westernized cultural context as the one of Soa Tome and Principe. This was still being done despite World Bank's evaluation unit findings that reveal that only 25 per cent of institutional development or public sector management projects could be judged even moderately successful. A 1991 review of technical assistance for institutional development found that the bulk of this assistance failed to make significant impact and was of doubtful sustainability (UNDP 1993: 220).

Even under the best circumstances, administrative reforms are high risk and long term enterprises. In the case of Sao Tome and Principe where a political campaign was starting and the prospects of salary reform were low, the generalized institutional weakness of the public sector will continue to hobble capacity-building effort.

PART V

ETHICS AND DEVELOPMENT IN THE UNITED STATES

Several scholars have made the point that development administration is not necessarily a process that takes place within international comparative administration. Indeed, some of the same stresses that come into play in developing countries in their dealing with powerful foreign donors, are present in U.S. state and local governments in their fiscal relationship with the federal government. The first of the two chapters of Part V reviews the process of development administration in the setting of an industrialized country.

The Immigration and Naturalization Service (INS) estimates that 1,9 percent of the current U.S. population – about five million people – are illegal immigrants, and 350,000 of them live in Florida. This figure represents 2.44 percent of the state population. These immigrants had an extraordinary impact on the economy of South Florida and on the service delivery capability of local service delivery. Chapter 10 focuses on five public service sectors that have carried the major burden of helping the immigrants: Welfare, Housing, Public Health, Education, and Law Enforcement. It is based on analysis of census data, South Florida public service reports, and interviews with public employees. It also projects future trends and comes up with some innovative designs to improve the delivery services to immigrants in South Florida public sector. The findings bring ideas for overcoming present obstacles to a better delivery system and suggest solutions for solving some of the problems arising from drastic budget cuts at the state and city levels and from a severe reduction in federal funding for the settlement of new immigrants. A tentative model is drawn to guide other public services that are affected by this kind of changing demographics.

The last chapter of the book looks at how the impact of technology makes human interaction increasingly complicated. The age of new technology and computers brings with it unparalleled dilemmas and a formidable challenge for government regulators. New technologies have developed faster than projected and have aroused great expectations. But since the Internet is practically "citizen-controlled," it presents an unusual challenge to government control. Today, the internet is a civic market place that evolved rapidly from a means for sharing resources and exchanging messages and documents, into a reference medium where research papers can be read by anyone in the network. When the World Wide Web was developed in 1990, it brought the Internet into the consumer marketplace. In the late 1990s, more than 15 million North American households have some kind of on-line access. In the year 2000, this figure has increased to 38 million. The large audience-network is in need of regulation in two special area: cryptology – the scrambling of a message which can only be decrypted if a receiver has the encryption key – and advertising, providing users with a place to research products, chat rooms to discuss these products, and in many cases the consumer can even buy the product on-line. Several ethical issues related to cryptology and advertising in the Internet will be addressed in this chapter. These are linked because only consumers' confidence in new encryption techniques will make them willing to put more and more of their spending and consumption patterns into databases. The chapter will discuss the advantages and disadvantages of having government regulate cryptology (national security and law enforcement vs. personal privacy and possible misuse of information accessed by the government) and advertising (the selling of goods and services backed by reliable research vs. crackpot theories masquerading as facts). The chapter will also suggest how government regulators can establish the delicate balance between these dilemmas without violating traditional administrative ethics. This is one of the great challenges they are facing in this new millennium.

10

THE IMPACT OF NEW IMMIGRANTS'
NEEDS ON SOUTH FLORIDA
PUBLIC SERVICE

In the early 1970's Haitians fleeing the disastrous political and economic conditions in their country started to cross the windward passage separating them from South Florida in flimsy sail boats. Their successful arrival encouraged hundreds of thousands other poor Haitians to undertake that dangerous journey in the following years. Between 1991 and 1994 tens of thousands additional Haitians fled political repression and economic hardship during the three years of military rule and international sanctions that ended in September 1994 when U.S. troops disarmed the Haitian army and restored democracy. When the Sandinistas took over the government of Nicaragua in 1979, hundreds of thousands also left that country and most of them came to South Florida. Finally, in 1980, 125,000 Cubans were permitted by Fidel Castro to go to South Florida from the port of Mariel to join the growing Cuban exile community there. These waves of new immigrants, some of them illegal, others granted asylum or refugee status, had an extraordinary impact on the economy of South Florida and on the service delivery capability of local public services (Hann 1991).

A report of the city of Miami shows that one of every three Miami residents in the early 1990's residents lives below the federal poverty line; one of every eight dwellings in the city is so rundown it should be demolished; and the average income of Miami residents has dropped almost 5 percent over the last decade. Detailed 1990 Census data showed that trends apparent in the 1980 Census have worsened. The City of Miami Community Development Department stated that the situation is due in large part to the influx of the new arrivals (1992; 1993).

The bleak economic picture has other repercussions. Ethnic/racial tensions are exacerbated as intense competition develops for existing housing, services and jobs, especially between lower income Americans and the new immigrants.

This chapter will focus on five public service sectors that have carried the major burden of helping the immigrants: Welfare, Housing, Public Health, Education, and Law Enforcement. It will be based on analysis of census data, South Florida public service reports, and interviews with public employees. It will also project future trends and come up with some innovative designs to improve the delivery of services to immigrants in South Florida public sector. The findings will bring ideas for overcoming present obstacles to a better delivery system and suggest solutions for solving some of the problems arising from drastic budget cuts at the state and city levels and from a severe reduction in federal funding for the settlement of the new immigrants. A tentative model will be drawn to guide other public services that are affected by this kind of changing demographics.

IMMIGRANTS IN SOUTH FLORIDA

The largest immigrant group counted by the Census Bureau in 1990 was the Cubans. The half-million Cuban-born people in Florida represent two-thirds of the entire country's Cuban-born population. The state is home to more than a third of the whole country's Haitian-born population. Haitians accounted for 4.7 percent of the immigrants in Florida, ranking third after the Cubans (28.2 percent) and the Canadians (4.8 percent) (Stepick and Stepick 1990; Stepick 1992). About 74,000 people in the Miami area claimed Nicaraguan ancestry. Census figures form 1990 show that more than 130,000 people in the Miami area speak languages other than Spanish and English at home. Since the 1980 Census, Spanish replaced English as the language most often spoken at home.

The immigration explosion of the 1980's, dramatized by the Mariel boatlift, the Nicaraguan exodus and the flight of Haitian boat people, has dramatically changed the demographics of South Florida. The area was transformed , swept by more change in the past decade than any other region in the country. As a result of this, income gaps are growing especially in Miami. According to an August 7, 1992 Miami Herald review of the 1990 Census, the city of Miami's make up is 49.2 percent Hispanic, 20.5 percent black and 30.2 percent non-Hispanic whites. But the percentage of Cuban-Americans within the Hispanic population is winding, from 80 percent in the 1970's to more than 60 percent at the present time. The 1990 Census shows that Hispanics made enormous gains in Dade's marketplace during the 1980's and that women also made large strides during that period, increasing their share of executive jobs in the county by 10 percentage points, to 42 percent. That mirrored a national trend. However, the picture was quite grim for blacks. Though the number of black men and women in executive jobs increased, they remain vastly under-represented in top positions and over-represented in menial jobs. The Whites who are still living in Dade often hold high-prestige jobs. They dominate trades like the law, science and aviation engineering.

The waves of international immigration in the 1980's had an uneven impact on two of South Florida's largest counties. According to the Miami Herald August 6, 1992 article, it made Dade less affluent and Broward wealthier. Broward, with a healthy base of retirees and benefiting to some degree, from flight out of Dade, has a per capita income of $16,883, 15 percent above Florida's average of $14,698. Broward's median household income of $30,571 puts it 11 percent above the state average. The Dade figures reveal a metropolitan area clearly having trouble sustaining its economic stature. Dade's per capita income of $13,686 is 7 percent below the state average and an enormous 20 percent below Broward's. Its median household income of $26,909 is 12 percent below Broward's and slightly below the state average. These figures from the 1990 Census show that poverty rates are sharply higher in Dade where 17.9 percent of the population fall below the poverty rate of an annual income of $14,040 for a family of four. Only 10.2 percent in Broward and 9 percent of the state's residents fall below that rate.

Because of the new economic situation, a growing number of Floridians seem to be intolerant toward the rise of immigration. Their attitudes reflect a national trend. This is revealed in a March 3, 1992 Miami Herald report of a Gallup poll in which 69 percent of the respondents said that too many immigrants were entering the United States.

The Cubans

The state of Florida has been able to cope with the influx of nearly one million Cuban refugees since 1959. A multibillion dollar federal aid program and the establishment of a strong, social, economic and political enclave in Miami has effectively facilitated the group's adaptation (Masud-Piloto 1988: 11). In February 1961, the U.S. government established a Cuban Refugee Program to ease the demographic and economic pressures that the influx of Cubans was exerting on South Florida. A resettlement program was set up to give assistance to the families arriving from Cuba if they immediately relocated away from Miami. The assistance included transportation costs to the new destination, help in finding housing and employment, and financial assistance until they could find a job. Between 1961 and 1978, 300,232 persons were resettled to New York, New Jersey, California and Illinois, a total representing 64 percent of all Cubans arriving in the United States and registering with the Cuban Refugee Program and 37 percent of all Cubans living in the United States in 1980 (Perez 1992: 87). During seven months in 1980 more than 125,000 arrived at Key West aboard a flotilla of boats in an exodus that became known as the Mariel boatlift. This massive migration created an enormous problem for the state of Florida but its impact on South Florida public service was limited because of two factors: the federal government's willingness to assume responsibility for the cost of their settlement and the aid contributed by the earlier Cuban immigrants, many of whom had become successful entrepreneurs (Cart 1990; Diaz 1985).

In 1992, the U.S. Coast Guard rescued 2,565 Cubans, the highest number since the Mariel boatlift. Today, new immigrants continue to flow in. The new immigrants were helped by a series of South Florida agencies that operate under government contracts. Most of these agencies expect the flow of refugees in 1993 to equal or even surpass last year's. This is due to the fact that the Cuban economy is at its worst point since the revolution. The Castro government does not seem able to cope without the massive aid that the former Soviet Union was giving. The internal situation has deteriorated to such an extreme that more and more Cubans are risking their lives to leave the island.

In the meantime, the U.S. federal government is slashing funding for a 15-year-old program that helps Cuban and Haitian refugees settle in the United States. Under the program the government pays the resettlement agencies to provide limited cash help, temporary housing, food, clothing and other assistance to Cuban and Haitian refugees. The agencies also provide referrals that help the refugees find jobs and schooling. But the U.S. Congress has been slow in the appropriation of proper funding for the program, leaving South Florida public service in a state of continuous financial crisis. Two new laws recently signed by President Clinton will make it even more difficult for immigrants to settle in the United States. Both the Anti-Terrorism and Effective Death Penalty Act, signed into law on April 24, 1996, and the Illegal Immigration Reform and Immigrant Responsibility Act, signed on September 30, 1996, directly or indirectly will adversely affect the settlement of immigrants.

In December 1996, the Immigration and Naturalization Service determined that Cuban refugees unlawfully reaching U.S. soil will be returned. The Cuban government still has to approve their return before they can be sent back. For the first time since Castro took over almost four decades ago, Cubans are now being treated as are all illegal entrants from other countries.

The Haitians

Haiti's economic and political situations steadily deteriorated throughout the late 1950's and early 1960's. A series of natural disasters — five hurricanes and three floods — nearly ruined the Haitian economy. Loss of direct American aide when Francois Duvalier declared himself President-for-Life in 1963, coupled with a slump in tourism and coffee and sisal prices did nothing to alleviate the situation. Haiti in the 1970's showed little hope of economic or political improvement. Chronic unemployment, augmented by capital-intensive rather than labor superficial liberalization of the regime, growing population pressures, and severe and prolonged droughts in 1975 and 1977, all fostered the outward flow during this period. The migration from Haiti has not abated since then (Buchanan 1980).

Soon after the first democratically elected President was sent into exile by the Haitian military in 1991, the Organization of American States invoked an economic embargo of Haiti. Life there was already very hard for a vast majority of the people. The embargo created such an extreme economic depravation for poor Haitians who were barely surviving that many of them found the risky boat trip to South Florida more attractive (Stepick 1992).

Nearly 40,000 Haitians have fled Haiti since the military coup of September 1991. Most of them were returned to Haiti by the Coast Guard. Some were temporarily housed in tent camps in the U.S. base in Guantanamo, Cuba, while Haitian refugee groups in the U.S. were mounting a legal challenge to the repatriation order. When these efforts failed in the courts those in Guantanamo were also returned except for a few hundred who were found to have a valid claim for asylum petition. As a candidate, Bill Clinton vowed to change U.S. processing of the asylum claims of Haitian boat people but the prospect of a Haitian version of the Mariel boatlift frightened South Florida and forced Clinton to continue his predecessor's policy to summarily return the Haitians to their country without processing their asylum claims. To make sure that the message will be understood in Haiti, a barrier of U.S. Coast Guard vessels was deployed around the Haitian coast (Stepick 1992: Florida Department of Health and Rehabilitative Services 1992).

The policy of persecution, legal confusion, and social isolation have all contributed to the dismal socio-economic conditions of Haitians in the U.S. Their employment situation compares unfavorably to any other immigrant population in the country. In 1985, involuntary employment was 24 percent. For those who were working, their places of employment were overwhelmingly apparel and furniture factories, restaurants and hotels where they were hired to perform the most menial tasks (Stepick 1992: 67).

Haitian refugees are rarely employed by other Haitians in sharp contrast with the Cubans. Forty-five percent of the Mariel refugees who were working were employed by other Cubans while only one percent of Haitian refugees were employed by other Haitians in 1983 (Ibid: 68).

After the restoration of democracy in Haiti in 1994, the federal government resumed its previous policy of returning all newly-arrived illegal Haitians to their country. Since then, the exodus has dropped dramatically.

The Nicaraguans

When Somoza of Nicaragua was defeated by the Sandinistas in 1979, several thousand Nicaraguans followed him into exile in Miami. This first group, known as the hard-liners, was soon followed by professionals and skilled workers, complaining of declining salaries and/or too much interference. They came to South Florida as tourists and stayed. By the mid-1980's, teen-age draft-dodgers were arriving because their parents feared that they would be killed in combat with CIA-backed Contra rebels. Despite the growing flow of Nicaraguans fleeing their country because of the war, no immigration reform measures were taken by the U.S. government. Instead, in June 1985, the U.S. Congress approved $27 million to continue the Reagan administration's efforts to overthrow the Sandinista government (Masud-Piloto 1988).

Nicaragua presented a particularly difficult problem for the U.S. federal government's immigration policy. Although the administration openly financed and supported the Sandinistas' enemies, Nicaragua was not a Communist nation and still had diplomatic relations with the United States. Thus when Nicaraguans claiming to be fleeing Sandinista repression applied for political asylum in the United States, their cases had to be reviewed individually. The Immigration and Naturalization Service was presented with a difficult dilemma (Ibid.).

By mid-1988, peasants and the urban poor, the revolution's chief beneficiaries, were arriving in South Florida. The exile community was no longer of one class or mind. When the Sandinistas lost the February 1990 elections, most Nicaraguan refugees decided not to return home. Those who had money to invest in the Nicaraguan economy had lost their properties. Those properties included several thousand homes. The Sandinista government had enacted a law that granted legal titles to those properties to their occupants. However, getting home was not easier for the Nicaraguans who wanted to do so because they have found it difficult to work or save money in the United States. The U.S. government had proposed an allocation of $47 million to assist the Contras to repatriate from neighboring Central American countries, but no funds to assist Nicaraguans in the United States to return home. Again, like in the cases of the Cubans and the Haitians, the state of Florida was left with the full responsibility for helping the Nicaraguans (Grenier and Stepick 1992).

Despite the second consecutive democratic election of a president who was installed in January 1997, the Nicaraguan population in South Florida will continue to grow. Nicaragua is still the second-poorest country in the hemisphere after Haiti. It also has one of the world's highest debt burdens and an unemployment rate that exceeds 50 percent.

THEIR IMPACT ON
PUBLIC SERVICE

Census figures from 1990 revealed that South Florida's work force underwent many changes. In Dade, the class of workers growing the most during the decade of the 1980's was state government employees. The increase in the size of the bureaucracy is directly linked to the increase in the number of people who are seeking government assistance and services. Another impact of the new immigrants on the public sector has been the increase in the number of Hispanics who joined the government bureaucracy because they were needed for service delivery. Following is a review of the five public service sectors that have carried the major burden of helping the immigrants: Welfare, Housing, Public Health, Education, and Law Enforcement.

Welfare

Immigrant participation in the welfare system has never been fully studied. It has been pointed out that the conflict between immigration and the existence of a welfare state raises questions of fundamental importance for social policy. There is a widespread perception that unskilled immigrants are particularly prone to enter the welfare system, and that the entry of large numbers of these immigrants in the past two decades has raised taxpayer expenditures on income transfer programs (Borjas and Trejo 1991: 195).

The Haitians and the Nicaraguans have been a greater burden to the South Florida welfare agencies than the Cubans. Although in 1960 as many as 50 percent of the Cuban exiles were receiving welfare benefits, by the end of 1966 only ten percent received welfare. The rate of unemployment among Cubans is also the lowest. Most Cubans would prefer to take any type of job rather than apply for welfare. In most communities where Cubans have settled, welfare officials have noted the powerful urge to stay off the relief rolls whenever jobs were available (Gallagher 1980: 51-52). Enough Cuban exiles organizations now exist in South Florida to substantially help the rafters.

Both the Haitians and the Nicaraguans do not have the extensive exile network of the Cubans. The median earnings of the Haitians in South Florida are $680 per month, and the proportion receiving food stamps or other welfare support is just below 25 percent (Stepick 1992: 67). The Nicaraguans are slightly better off. The West Dade Community known as Little Managua has new schools, several trailer parks and shopping centers, a level of relative prosperity never enjoyed by the North Miami community known as Little Haiti.

Many of the South Florida immigrants have applied for political asylum. In most cases, the Immigration and Naturalization Service (INS) marks asylum applicants as eligible for eventual deportation. In such cases, Florida Department of Rehabilitative Services won't grant them Medicaid or AFDC payments. When an immigrant tried to challenge this policy in the Florida Supreme Court in 1992, the legislature passed a law to make sure that the welfare policy remains as is. Yet because of enormous backlogs (Miami's INS office alone has some 75,000 asylum applications pending), the process typically extends for years or even decades (Fix and Passel 1991; Grenier and Stepick 1992; U.S. Committee for Refugees 1991 and 1992).

The situation of the immigrants in South Florida will worsen because new federal welfare measures are now limiting welfare even for U.S. born citizens. Several hundred thousand welfare recipients are being forced to look desperately for jobs. New immigrants might be willing to work at jobs that apparently nobody wants but stiff penalties are being imposed on employers of illegal workers.

Housing

In 1991 the City of Miami published a report called The Comprehensive Housing Affordability Strategy that was sent to federal officials as part of the city's request for federal money for homeless programs or housing. The report stated that 31.1 percent of Miami's residents, or about 123,000 people, slipped below the federal poverty line in 1989 in large part because of the influx of refugees. Higher income groups moved out of the city, eroding its tax base. That left Miami with little money for economic revitalization and to invest in economic development. The report estimated that 21 percent of the city's dwellings needed rehabilitation. More than half of those have deteriorated so much they cannot be saved. Twelve percent of the city's housing stock, or nearly 16,790 dwellings, should be razed according to the report (City of Miami 1991).

According to the 10th annual survey on hunger and homelessness conducted by the U.S. Conference of Mayors and released in December 1992, Miami has one of the most severe problems with homeless and hungry people in the nation, as the city faces a 40 percent increase in demand for emergency food and has shelter space for only a third of those who need it. According to the survey, requests for assisted housing in Miami has a wait of 30 months.

Cubans have competed more successfully for housing in South Florida than the Nicaraguans and the Haitians. Their success has been due to the relative prosperity of a large number of Cubans who are able to invest some of their own money into helping the Cuban community. Some of the agencies that assist Cubans in need are totally financed by successful Cubans.

Public Health

A great majority of the new immigrants to South Florida lack health insurance. Cubans are more likely to be insured than Nicaraguans and Haitians because they are better educated and have higher incomes than the other two groups. The Exodus Program, created in 1988, has brought 8,500 Cuban refugees stuck in third countries to the United States to join friends and family. As part of the program, the Cuban American National Foundation helped arrange for private health insurance for all Exodus refugees for two years. Other measures were also taken by the Foundation to make sure that the refugees would not become public charges. Given their high employment rates, in general, most of the Cuban Americans are better off than other Hispanics. However, according to a Miami Herald article of December 19, 1991, the private agencies that help refugees have had a real problem in gaining medical access for the Nicaraguans and the Haitians. One solution for the refugees who cannot afford private health insurance could be Medicaid. But in Florida, they cannot get Medicaid because of stringent state eligibility criteria .

Individual Nicaraguan doctors have established special arrangements to treat patients for common illnesses at a flat monthly rate. The Haitian Health Foundation is one of several groups working to make medical care accessible to more people in the Haitian community. A 1989 report commissioned by Dade County said that more than half of the residents of Little Haiti never see a doctor. The Haitian Health Foundation has been able to come up with an estimated $1 million to rent a facility and offer pediatric care, dental services, a women's health section, social workers and health education programs. Several Haitian physicians are also involved with other facilities to promote vision care and other health services among Haitian immigrants.

New federal health regulations may soon force public hospitals and clinics to ask each patient's immigrant status. Such measures could keep some illegal immigrants away, allowing contagious diseases to go unchecked. This has triggered a new public debate about government's obligation to tend to immigrants, the poor and the general public health, a huge challenge for South Florida.

Education

The exodus of Cubans in the 1960's brought thousands of refugee children and presented South Florida's schools with their first experience with children who had been raised speaking a foreign language, in a system totally different from the American one. The first influx allowed the local, state and federal officials to work out programs to incorporate the refugees into the mainstream of American Society in a systematic way. By 1962, the Dade County Public Schools had established bilingual programs and special curricula had been developed to help the new students make the transition from one language to another without holding back their academic progress in all subjects. But in 1980 after the Mariel Boatlift brought in at once a massive number of children of school age, the Dade County Public Schools received a $1 million grant for a special summer program for 5,000 children. The program ended up serving 9,000 children and the $1 million took ten months to reach the strained Dade schools system (Dade County Public Schools, Office of Educational Accountability 1984; 1992a; and 1992b).

But hiring Spanish-speaking teachers was just the beginning for South Florida public schools. The number of Haitian children arriving there grew considerably in the 1980's and they presented a new challenge to the system. At the present time Dade schools employ 35 to 40 Creole-speaking teachers. Several refugee agencies first teach the new students "English as a second language" and give them tips on how to survive in America before they enroll in the school system. A great number of the Haitian students come from Haiti's rural, hilly provinces where electricity and indoor plumbing are rare. But the values of the peasant class in Haiti are the same as the American middle class. They want to have a good job when they grow up and they understand that the only way to make it is to go to school and complete their studies. Most of them would have never grown up to have a good social-economic position if they have stayed in Haiti. They fully realize that education is the great elevating and equalizing force of American society. Margaret Mead once commented that the greatest travesty in American education was making everyone think he not only needed a college education but was entitled to one. The young immigrants fully understand that the only way to college education is the arduous years in the public schools (Ibid.).

During the school year 1991-92, 142,145 of Dade schools' students were Hispanic (46.7 percent), 102,218 were Black (33.6 percent), and 59,924 were White (19.7 percent). These figures were obtained from the Dade County Public Schools student database system. But they don't show the number of foreign students enrolled in the system. Figures for the previous year, 1990-91, reveal that 12,755 students were from 95 other countries. The highest number came from Haiti (1,763) followed by Nicaragua (1,703) and Cuba (1,696). These three countries had a total of 5,162 students enrolled, or 40 percent of all foreign students. For the year 1990-91, Educational Research Service, Inc. computed the budgeted current expenditures per pupil in twenty of the largest U.S. districts. Their data show that Dade County was spending $5,418 per pupil that year. At that cost, the amount of money spent by the school system for educating students from other countries in 1991-92 was a steep $69,106,590 dollars. These expenses are mandatory by law. In 1982, the United States Supreme Court in a 5-4 ruling ordered public schools to educate the children of undocumented aliens (Ibid.).

Law Enforcement

No definite study exists that shows a direct link between the number of immigrants entering South Florida and the growing crime rate there. But there is little doubt that immigration contributes to tensions among diverse groups. Those tensions sometimes foster stereotyping and trigger heated reactions to ethnic issues. Hate crimes are flourishing all across South Florida. Sometimes they involve Anglos and Hispanics but very often it is Blacks against Hispanics or even Blacks against Haitians.

According to a Miami Herald article of January 24, 1992, one of the most violent confrontations between police and Haitian demonstrators took place in 1990 and might have been avoided if a dispute between a Cuban merchant and a Haitian customer had not been allowed to grow into an ethnic-political issue. U.S. Census figures reveal that a decade of rising crime made security work South Florida's fastest growing occupation. The number of police, fire fighters, jail guards and private security officers leaped by 74 percent in 10 years to over 50,000.

A poll released in June 1992 found that 75 percent of Florida residents believe race relations are poor or only fair. But the poll also found that about half of Whites and Blacks feel that the police treat Blacks and Whites the same (Institute for Public Opinion Research 1992). Despite these findings, there is ample evidence that race relations have been at the base of many incidents involving the police and the immigrants. In an article on police corruption in Miami the two authors focused on cases involving drug trafficking and drug-related cases but clearly illustrated the dim racial climate that exists in South Florida (Sechrest and Burns 1992). Two other authors found that the crimes of recent immigrants in South Florida create a type of crime problem not characteristic of most U.S. metropolitan areas. It is a type of crime that lacks integration between the conventional and criminal value systems. They pointed out that strangely, most American crime is integrated into the conventional system, enough so that it is structured and controlled to some degree (Dunham and Werner 1991: 97).

Thus, the challenges presented to law enforcement agencies in South Florida by the new immigrants go well beyond the budgetary implications of their presence, it also obliges them to train their officers in both foreign languages and foreign cultures.

LESSONS LEARNED AND
SOME SOLUTIONS

Although the population changes occurring in South Florida are more dramatic than in other urban areas of the country, they somewhat mirror what the United States could be in the mid-21st Century. According to a Miami Herald article of December 4, 1992, after the 1990 Census was taken and analyzed, the U.S. Census Bureau's look at the country in the year 2,050 is that there will be 128 million more people than there are today. One in five will be Hispanic, Asians will be steadily gaining in numbers on Blacks, and non-Hispanic Whites will be dropping from 75 percent of the population to just more than half. This changing portrait of America already exists in South Florida. In a Miami Herald article of April 19, 1992, some Latin Americans, after visiting Miami, were quoted as saying that they chose the city "because it is almost like America."

Other communities that are experiencing the kind of changing demograph-ics occurring in Miami could draw a tentative model from some of the solutions found there. The actions taken in Miami originated from both the public sector and the new immigrants' private sector. However, Miami's Cubans are probably more capable of imitating such conciliatory actions than immigrant groups in other cities. The Cubans in South Florida have achieved economic and political power without, it seems, paying the customary price of assimila-tion. Following are three actions that exemplify the spirit of cooperation between South Florida's public service and the emerging immigrant sector.

Neighborhood City Halls

Miami government has often been criticized for being too remote to the people it serves, especially the ethnic neighborhoods where the immigrants live. To address this problem, it is developing an elaborate plan to open satellite city halls in many of these neighborhoods. According to the plan, police officers will be stationed there and will go around on foot knocking on doors, learning about a community, and helping neighborhoods protect themselves. The officers will be based in the community, along with a cadre of code inspectors, city planners and job training specialists. Miami is planning 8 to 15 of these "mini city halls." The present city management forecasts that it will be a radical change in the way of delivering services. Many large cities, including New York, have already embarked on community policing but most of their programs bear the imprint of a police reform movement sweeping the country. Those programs focus on police activities and do not cover the larger array of city services that will be brought in to the communities. In Miami, each neighborhood city hall will be staffed, at a minimum, by an administrator who will run the office, a police officer, a fire department representative, a planner and a code inspector.

Bureaucratic Empowerment

While the rate of Hispanic hirings at federal and state level has risen steadily in the last decade, it has not kept pace with the rise in Hispanic population. By the latest count, there are 1,830,300 executive branch employees, of whom 114,740 are Hispanic. This makes the U.S. government America's largest and most diverse employer (Minorities and Women 1998). The 395-member District of Columbia Council of Hispanic Employment managers was organized in 1970 by managers of Hispanic employment programs from various government agencies. The group stages job fairs every month to insure that Hispanics have equal opportunities at federal employment. Likewise, Hispanics are significantly under-represented in Metropolitan Dade County's work force. In 1991, the National Association of Hispanic Public Administrators undertook a comprehensive analysis of Dade's personal activity (1991). The data from the report was drawn from Metropolitan Dade County reports, and employment reports from City of Miami as well as the 1990 Census (Metro-Dade Planning Department, Research Division 1988; City of Miami 1992 and 1993).

The report indicates that Hispanics trail behind the community's representation by 18.9 percent and are under-represented by 4,156 in Metro-Dade's work force. Efforts in reducing the gap made some progress. In FY 1989-90, a total of 40.9 percent of all new appointments were Hispanics. In terms of volume, the largest number of new appointments totaling 570 went to Hispanics. By comparison, new appointments for White non-Hispanics totaled 373 and 421 for Blacks (Metro-Dade Planning Department, Research Division 1988; National Association of Hispanic Public Administrators 1991; City of Miami 1992 and 1993)..

The report also classified the Dade government positions into four categories: officials and administrators, professionals, office/clerical and protective services. In the category of officials and administrators Hispanics had 209 positions (21.1 percent), Blacks had 202 (20.4 percent) and Whites had 568 (57.3 percent). Some disparity also existed between males and females in this class. Males made up 67.2 percent and females 35.4 with Hispanic females accounting for 6.3 percent of this classification (National Association of Hispanic Public Administrators 1991; Metro-Dade Planning Department, Research Division 1988; City of Miami 1992 and 1993).

Among the professionals the number of Hispanics were 1,070 (30.4 percent). The Whites had 1,448 positions (41.1 percent) and the Blacks 928 (26.3 percent). The disparity was even greater in the protective services category where Whites had 2,478 positions (49 percent), Blacks, 1,279 (25.3 percent) and Hispanics, 1,260 (24.9 percent). Not surprisingly the Whites were the minority only in the clerical category where there were1,260 (25.8 percent) versus 1,698 blacks (36.3 percent) and 1,679 Hispanics (35.9 percent) (National Association of Hispanic Public Administrators 1991).

An equally important measurement of parity is salary distribution. An analysis of income indicated that minorities and females trailed behind White non-Hispanic males. In the salary range of $60,000 and above, White non-Hispanics made up 78 percent of the distribution. Similar statistics were indicative of the $43,000 to $59,000 income group. While minorities were under-represented in the high salary positions, they were over-represented in the lower side of the scale. Black participation in particular made up a large percentage of low paying jobs (National Association of Hispanic Public Administrators. 1991).

Although the analysis of Metro Dade's personnel activity by ethnicity and gender implicated uneven representations and deficiencies, the figures were much higher than the federal ones and those of other communities with large groups of immigrants. Two factors account for this. First of all, most of the Hispanics in the public service in South Florida are Cuban Americans and as a group they are above the other newly arrived immigrants in educational and economic terms. The other factor is the fact that most of the Cuban-Americans benefited from special consideration that allowed them to become legal residents and later U.S. citizens, soon after their arrival. No other groups of immigrants had achieved such success as quickly in the history of immigration in the United States. In South Florida, the two other large groups of immigrants, the Haitians and the Nicaraguans will probably follow the traditional pattern of previous immigrant groups and will have to wait one or two generations to be able to claim equitable representation in the public service. Their biggest stumbling blocks to bureaucratic empowerment at the time are their lack of education and citizenship.

An Hispanic Round Table

Miami has several associations of civic and business leaders that usually meet to discuss community issues. The most prominent one is more than twenty years old and is dominated by the business establishment. Most members are non-Hispanic whites. The newest association — La Mesa Redonda (The Round Table) — is made up of seventeen of Dade's most powerful Hispanic leaders: 15 Cuban American men, one Nicaraguan American man and one Cuban American woman. They run many of Dade's largest public institutions. They lead banks, newspapers, corporations and broadcast stations. Some are public officials. All are members of the city's new elite. They are riding the crest of the demographic changes sweeping South Florida. Their goal is to make a difference in Miami and to help the Hispanic community.

In 1992, less than eighteen months after its formation, the Hispanic Round Table had the governor of the state as their guest in one of their monthly diners. In a Miami Herald article of April 29, 1992, a spokesman for the group told the governor that there were too few Hispanics in prominent posts in the administration and the governor should push for more Hispanic representation in new legislative districts.

Officially, the members of the Round Table never discuss their agenda in public. Some have hinted that it is a mere discussion group not organized to prompt any kind of action. They say that it is organized to allow a group of friends to meet once a month to talk about community concerns in Spanish, their native tongue. But when a member of the group became deeply involved in efforts to help Jackson Memorial Hospital — the primary facility used by immigrants — he emphasized the importance of a half-cent sales tax for medical care at Jackson. After months of cajoling by the Round Table members and others, Hispanic voters, with a long track record of voting against taxes, went to the polls in September 1991 and voted in favor of this one. It passed, ensuring $60 million a year for the crowded hospital.

CONCLUSIONS

South Florida's immigration patterns are unique in many ways. No other part of the country has received such continuous flows of immigrants over such a limited period of time. The ones who arrived in the early 1960's contributed greatly to the transformation of metropolitan Miami from a sleepy heaven for retirees into a dynamic cosmopolitan center. But ethnic pride was exalted at the expense of social cohesion. While prior generations of immigrants had to learn English quickly to survive, many Hispanics maintain that the Spanish language is inseparable from their ethnic and cultural identity, and seek to remain bilingual, if not primarily Spanish speaking. The 1990 U.S. Census statistics revealed that the rest of the state of Florida is rapidly becoming more like South Florida. It has whole new urban areas and whole new demographics. Data compiled from the 1990 Census shows that Florida has become more urban, more crowded, better educated and far more diverse in population. The conversion of Florida's farmland to suburbia continues unabated and the building boom is simply unprecedented.

However, in the mist of the apparent march toward progress wide social and educational disparities remain. The gap between the "haves" (usually non-Hispanic Whites and wealthy Hispanics) and the "have nots" (the Blacks, poor Hispanics and a large portion of the immigrants) seem to be growing rapidly. This uneven social, political and economic development is common in large urban centers but in South Florida it has more of the flavor of Third World inequities. The only difference is the fact that South Florida public service agencies are working harder to solve the problems. Ironically, they face the very same type of restrictions as the ones faced by Third World bureaucracies: budgetary ones.

A segment of the population of South Florida resists the immigration waves. Many do not think that a state going through such a major economic crisis and deprived of an income tax base will ever be able to employ vast number of new people, house them, educate them, protect them in their old age, and provide them health care. Unfortunately, in South Florida as in other places where refugees are numerous, there seems to be an excessive emphasis on the big negatives that stir up emotions. Too little attention is given to the day-to-day process of integration. Some of the facts seldom mentioned by the critics are that many of these immigrants work and pay taxes, and that their presence creates a link with other countries, a great asset for South Florida's business relations.

Refugee protection and assistance are fundamentally federal government responsibilities. But it has been extremely difficult for Florida to ensure federal reimbursement of the adverse economic impacts on their budget. Unfortunately the U.S. federal government does not have an adequate plan to deal with immigration emergencies of the kind that South Florida experienced with the massive influx of Cubans, Haitians, and Nicaraguans. Federal reimbursement of state and local costs related to an emergency remains unclear. Congress created a $35 million emergency fund in 1987 — $20 million of which can go to state and local governments — but rules to dispense the money have never been finalized. A major weakness of the existing federal plan is that it overlooks any effort to prevent the type of immigration crisis that South Florida has been experiencing over the past thirty years. Critics think that the federal government should be encouraged to continuously pursue all diplomatic avenues available to avoid a mass immigration influx. Given the anxiety over deteriorating conditions in Cuba, Haiti and Nicaragua, these critics feel that federal planners are not taking the threat of a refugee emergency in South Florida seriously enough.

11

ETHICAL ISSUES IN THE USE
OF THE INTERNET

At its beginning in 1969, the Internet was a technology-and-communications network for the United States Defense Department and for university researchers. By 1996 it had grown into a colossus connecting 52 million of the world's 234 million computers. It serves as everything from a personal playground to an information superhighway for businesses. The formation of a global network society (a world in which people, businesses and institutions are linked by interconnected computers) is fast becoming a reality. At the present time, only one percent of the world's population is using a personal computer, and even a smaller number connected to the Internet. But some estimates predict that the world will have at least one billion cybercitizens connected to the Internet by the year 2008. However, there are serious concerns over privacy, government regulation, taxation and whether some countries will ever keep pace with the early starters like the United States. So high is the concern over on-line privacy in the United States that 82 separate bills are pending in the U.S. Congress regarding privacy on-line. Similar legislation is either pending or already law in countries around the world (Sagan 1998: 45-46).

The age of technology and computers brings with it unparalleled dilemmas in the industrialized societies, especially in the United States. Three related ethical issues will be discussed in this chapter: cryptology, advertising and e-commerce on the Internet. These three issues will have great implications in the application of administrative ethics in the more advanced countries. But they also will affect the way the process of development administration will be carried out in the Third World Countries. As a matter of fact, this technology is making the concept of the "Global Village" more of a reality. After discussing some ethical problems involved with cryptology and advertising on the Internet, the difficulties of government regulations of these new technologies will be examined. Finally, their impact on development administration will be reviewed.

CRYPTOGRAPHY

The issue of cryptography, once a subject only spies and the military had any interest in, has become a hot topic because of its use on the Internet. The dilemma is one of security and privacy versus law enforcement and national security. Encryption policy is both essential for the growth of Internet commerce and vital for protection of privacy in the information age. As the battle is fought, questions of morality and ethics are seldom discussed. In the global world of computers, regulations are being established which must coincide with the establishment of global ethics.

Cryptography is the practice of coding messages so that they can only be read by the intended receiver. In the computer world, it is the scrambling of a message which can only be decrypted if the receiver has the encryption key.

The technology to encrypt messages on the Internet has been around for many years, but it has just within the past few years become an issue. One reason is that more and more sensitive transactions are occurring via the Internet. The problem is that people are increasingly entrusting information to computer, everything from confidential medical records to business plans to money itself. Something needs to be done to provide security so that these data will be protected from eavesdropper, thieves and saboteurs. Without encryption, anyone can read these messages and use them for illegal and unethical purposes. For one to read an encrypted message, one must either have the key or be able to decode the encryption.

The strength of the cryptography determines how easy it is to decode. The higher the bits in the key, the harder it is to crack. For instance, a 56 bit key is theoretically 65,000 times harder to crack than a 40 bit key. This is significant because as technology becomes more efficient, these codes become easier to crack with simple computers. In recent attacks on 40-bit exportable cryptography, any attacker with a moderate amount of computer power has been able to decrypt captured messages without access to an encryption key (Garfinkel 1996).

The argument for strong encryption in the business world is convincing. If people can gain unauthorized access to the kinds of information that are being transmitted, the result could be massive fraud and theft. The economic benefit of strong cryptography to business, therefore, is great.

The first argument that the United States government has against cryptography is that of national security. The export of strong cryptography to countries outside the United States has been banned because the government is afraid that the technology will be used against this country. The U.S. would no longer be able to decode certain information from other countries to which it currently has access. As explained by Simson L. Garfinkel, the author of the book PGP: Pretty Good Privacy, "the Government classifies encryption software as munitions, because foreign countries can use such programs to hide their communications during times of war." (1996: 15 (N) and 23 (L)) The result is that only weak cryptography systems are being made by U.S. manufacturers. Although they could sell strong encryption packages to customers within the U.S., it is not cost effective to manufacture two different products (Garfinkel 1996). Since software companies do not like to release two versions of their products, they offer a weaker version that is approved-for-export.

The second dilemma that cryptography presents to the government is one of law enforcement. Like the postal service and telephone system, there are times when illegal communication occurs and law enforcement officials feel they must have access to control it. Not only is there the potential for theft and fraud, but for child pornography, terrorism, drug deals etc. Law enforcement officials believe that with access to messages sent via the Internet, they can gather evidence regarding many criminal acts.

The government has proposed a system called a key escrow which would allow them access to encrypted information. The system they propose would allow people and companies to purchase and use strong cryptography as long as the key was held by a third party. This key would be available if the company lost access to their key or it could be used by law enforcement individuals if they first obtained a warrant.

There seem to be two main arguments against this system. The first is the fear of the government having access to private information. The idea of "Big Brother" having the ability to watch every Internet transaction is frightening to many people. Phil Zimmerman, who developed the Pretty Good Privacy (PGP) cryptography program, feels that people should have the freedom "to whisper something in someone's ear a thousand miles away." (Garfinkel 1996).

The second reason follows the first closely. It is that there is a fear that law officials could misuse the information they access. There is a feeling of general mistrust of the government. As writer Gary H. Anthes puts it "it boils down to whom you fear more: drug dealers, pedophiles and terrorists or the U.S. government." (1995: 66).

Most information recently published on this subject seems to be against government regulation of cryptography. In general, this appears to be because most people are acting under the theory of Egoism. If cryptography is not regulated, businesses can expand and become faster and more efficient. This would mean larger profits.

In determining a solution to the government's dilemma in dealing with cryptography, one should first separate industry from the individual computer user. In the case of business and industry, the ethical theory of Utilitarianism should be applied. The reason is that the issues here are of theft and fraud. They do not directly affect personal safety. Will cryptography eliminate misuse on the Internet, or will it enable businesses to circumvent the government? To solve this dilemma, government and business and industry must address these issues collectively. The solution lies in a system that can afford secure communications while allowing justified investigations.

Many people believe that the right to privacy is addressed in the Constitution of the United States. It is, however, more an issue of conventional morality. There are fewer laws encroaching on privacy. Think of the many states that used to have laws against certain sexual acts, even when they occurred in private between consenting adults. Though there are still some states that have these laws, they are seldom enforced. On the other hand, technology has allowed more glimpses into private lives than ever before. The ability to gain personal knowledge through the Internet must be brought into the open for discussion. Should the use of technology follow morality, or should morality be dictated by technological capabilities?

In addition, moral principles need to be applied when discussing privacy versus public safety issues. Freedom of speech does not allow for certain illegal discussion. Some examples of this would be soliciting for prostitution, threatening individuals, giving enemy nations classified information and distributing child pornography. These same laws need to be enforced even when the communication is taking place via the Internet. To allow these communications to occur because of the privacy of one individual is to violate the principles of respect for others.

And lastly, if the United States can educate law enforcement officials on ethical behavior, perhaps the mistrust that is now perceived towards these public officials would be alleviated. If they could be trusted to do their jobs according to Duty Ethics, the idea of a key escrow system would not be so scary.

The government regulation of cryptography is a hot subject. The decisions made about it will affect big businesses to government agencies to the personal computer user. In an age where technology is developed at such a rapid rate, time must be taken to develop ethical and moral standards that will protect the users. It is also important because in the rush to compete globally and gain larger profits, there must be respect for individuals. By applying ethical theories, government can help to insure this protection through regulation without harming the inevitable flow of information via the Internet.

ADVERTISING ON THE INTERNET

The Internet is rapidly becoming a marketplace where business is conducted. It provides users with advertising, a place to research products, chat rooms to discuss these products, and in many cases the consumer can even buy the product on-line. Though the Internet is not considered a mass media, yet, it will be in the near future. The number of people using it is growing at an unprecedented rate. Advertising and sales on the Internet, while providing increasing benefits to both businesses and consumers, are presenting ethical dilemmas as well. In this chapter, methods of advertising on the Internet will be explored as well as possible problems and issues as the technology and commercialism of the system grows.

The Internet provides a new medium for advertising products. As with television, radio, and print media, the Internet must be able to produce revenue in order to survive. Advertising has provided a method of generating revenue in other forms of mass media, so naturally companies have looked to this newest medium to advertise their products as well. There are several ways that a company may advertise on the Internet. Some of the most common forms include banners, commercial homepages, yellow pages, junk mail, push-oriented technology, and chat rooms.

Banners, like many forms of traditional advertising try to capture the customer's attention. Banners are typically found at the top of common web sites. The difference between a traditional attention-grabbing advertisements and banners are that with one click, the user can gain even more information about the product if they are interested in it. Something called hypertext is used on the Internet to let the user know that they can get additional information simply by clicking on the highlighted text, usually differentiated by a different color type. The hypertext links the user to another web site which contains more information promoting the product.

Popular web sites, like search engines and news magazines, sell banner space on their pages. Advertisers may buy banner space at different sites according to their audience, as well. A good example is a cruise line that buys banner space at America On Line's (AOL) Travel Reservation site. Different banners are alternated so that a user may see a different ad each time they open that particular page. Currently, this costs the advertiser two to five cents each time their banner is viewed (Advertising on the Internet 1998).

Another method of advertising is the Commercial Homepage. Most national companies now have a web site where their products are promoted. Everything from soda companies, to stock brokers, to universities now have homepages. These are web sites that are set up to promote and provide information about different products. They are primarily set up for consumers who want information about a specific brand product or who are browsing for a particular type of product (Electronic billboards 1998). For instance, a person who wants information about Florida International University can go straight to FIU's homepage, or a person wanting information about state universities in Florida could browse or search for "Florida State Universities" and see that FIU has a homepage.

Yellow Pages are now available on the Internet. These business directories can be found for specific localities or worldwide. Yellow pages are usually businesses listed by category which have links to homepages. They also may have phone numbers and addresses. Although the index may be free for businesses, yellow pages often sell banner space to make them profitable (Electronic billboards 1998).

Like regular mail, advertisers may also send information directly to your e-mail box. This can be done through bulk e-mail and by spamming. Advertisers can create or buy a list of potential customers and send promotional material straight to those Internet addresses. Spamming is a method of setting up an automatic reply so that the user receives an advertisement every time the user sends e-mail to a specific site. This method of unsolicited promotion or junk mail is frowned upon by most Internet users, but there are no general regulations against it. Some servers prohibit its use by their customers, however (SuperNet 1998).

According to Mitch Wagner in a February 24, 1997 article in Computerworld, one of the newest technologies which has advertising potential is push-oriented technology. If users want information about a product or service, they simply make a request via e-mail and the information is automatically sent to their e-mail address. This allows customers to request information without having to search for it. It is also advantageous to the advertiser because they take a more aggressive approach to reaching consumers). Rather than waiting for a user to find and browse the commercial homepage or web site, the advertiser takes an active role in getting the information to the user. Another advantage is that updated information can automatically be sent to the user and outdated information replaced. Currently, the system is being used mostly for software distribution and information dissemination, but the potential is there to expand the uses for any vendor on the Internet. In a February 3, 1997 article of Computerworld, for example, Wagner shows how Ford Motor Company is using it to send distributors information updates to help them sell cars.

One of the most useful ways that businesses can advertise is by word of mouth. The Internet provides its own forums for sharing information between users. Products often receive endorsements from users or paid promoters (Electronic billboard 1998). The users can e-mail friends or lists of people to get the word out. They can also enter chat rooms which allow people to interact electronically via their computers. Chat rooms are very popular on the Internet. Often they are set up by category or interest groups. A person wishing to buy a car, for instance, might enter a chat room on automobiles. More specifically, she/he could enter a room on a make, model, or style of car. They might find others who either have or are considering buying the same car. This allows people to compare notes and receive information from other consumers who are perfect strangers but have similar interests or areas of expertise.

Services like Compunet Services, Inc. are available to help advertisers maximize the use of all of the forms of promotion on the Internet. They assert that on-line advertising "is very cost effective, it offers exposure on a global scale, it is available 24 hours a day and has millions of users." Many such companies currently exist and the market for advertising sales is rapidly increasing (SuperNet 1998).

Another of the advantages of advertising on the Internet is the ability to sell the product on-line. Companies can advertise their products to users, provide in depth and relevant information about the product, and actually close the sale on the computer. Many industries are adding on-line sales to their current means of making their products accessible to consumers. A user can buy items such as airline tickets, groceries, and even cars on-line. And although some industries feel as though they cannot replace their human sales staff with a computer, there is definitely potential for this to occur in the not so distant future.

Most industries use credit cards for money transactions. In the future, however, there may be other methods of electronic commerce. Although this chapter will not go into depth about this topic, it is important to know that new technologies are being developed to make commerce on the Internet easier and more secure (Advertising on the internet 1998).

One U.S. government estimate predicts that e-commerce will grow into the trillions dollars annually by the year 2008. A good example of e-commerce performance is Intel Corporation, which sells computer chips through a website. Intel was aiming for more than one billion U.S. dollars in Internet sale in 1998. That came after the company discovered that an on-line effort to support large, existing accounts created an efficient new way to sell to thousand of customers who previously were too small to command the attention of a human salesperson. Over the web, Intel is interacting with small players and conducting tiny transactions with sufficient customer support at a cost low enough to sustain a new, profitable market. E-commerce can also have shockingly low overhead costs. Dell Computers reports that in every sale that the company makes over the Web, no employee is involved until an electronic order arrives at the factory, where a custom personal computer is assembled and shipped in a matter of hours (Sagan 1998: 46).

Another good example of what is being sold on the Internet is airline tickets. There are several airline reservation services offered through different servers on the World Wide Web. America On Line's service, for example, allows a user to type in their personal profile, including dates of travel and preferred airlines, and then lists available flights and costs. The user may buy the ticket by giving his or her credit card information.

Although many customers are already using on-line reservation services rather than travel agents, there are concerns about what can and cannot currently be offered on-line. According to Wagner's February 3, 1997 article in Computerworld, some airline deals are not available to users on the Internet. As the demand grows, and more customers use their computers to book their flights, the airlines will save money by advertising on-line and more deals will become available. Many customers are already using on-line reservation services rather than travel agents.

A good example of an industry that is struggling with what services to provide on the Internet is life insurance. According to a survey by Computer Sciences Corp (CSC) consumers prefer not to buy insurance on the Internet. Insurance relies on salespeople to get the customer to think about buying the product. Few people actually seek out information on life insurance. According to' Thomas Hoffman in a February 17, 1997 article in Computerworld, other arguments against on-line sales include that the information is too complex and that underwriters require medical information. Although these concerns may be valid today, in the future consumers can anticipate solutions which will make this type of interaction possible. Imagine advertising more like television, user-friendly information to explain the complexities, and the ability of the user to access verified medical records from a physician at the click of a button.

Another reason that many businesses are still wary of advertising on the Web is that they question whether they can reach enough people through the Internet to make a profit. Although the advertising may be inexpensive, building the information data bases, security, and increasing the general infrastructure of their system can become quite costly. According to Kathleen Gow, in a February 24, 1997 article in Computerworld Premier, there are other concerns such as legal questions, limited development tools, taxes and audit trails.

Also, the Internet is not yet considered a mass media. McGrath in Newsweek magazine on January 27, 1997, reported that "more than 15 million North American households had some form of on-line access. In the year 2000, the projection was that North America would have 38 million on-line households." McGrath further reported that analysts believe the critical mass to be about 30 million households, which suggests that the Web will become a true mass medium very soon. Even if these figures are off, it is safe to assume that the Internet will, in the near future, be a major source for reaching substantial volumes of people.

ETHICAL ISSUES AND DIFFICULTIES REGULATING THE INTERNET

With the incredible rate of increase in the use of the Internet, come several ethical dilemmas. As with any new technology, it is hard to predict all of the ramifications and issues that may arise. There are some that are already evident and need to be addressed, however. These ethical issues include freedom of speech, regulating advertising and sales, access, and the human element.

Although many Internet users want quick and easy access to information about products and services, they do not necessarily like the idea of on-line advertising. There is a general sentiment against regulations on the Internet, however, which means that they do not necessarily agree with banning businesses from advertising. This attitude is based upon the right to free speech which has been championed by computer users since the Internet was first used (Electronic billboards 1998). Currently, there are plenty of guidelines available for advertisers, but as of yet, few requirements. Part of the reason that this works so well is that unlike other media, the Internet is interactive. If users are unhappy with a product, service, or company, they have the potential to reach out to other customers worldwide and share their experience. It would not be worth it for a company to risk censure by a disgruntled customer who could potentially "talk" to thousands of other users (Electronic billboards 1998).

The American Marketing Association has a code of ethics for marketing on the Internet which addresses some of these issues. Their proscribed guidelines are as follows:

1. Support of professional ethics to avoid harm by protecting the rights of privacy, ownership, and access.

2. Adherence to all applicable laws and regulations with no use of Internet marketing that would be illegal if conducted by mail, telephone, fax, or other media.
3. Awareness of changes in regulations related to Internet marketing.
4. Effective communication to organizational members on risks and policies related to Internet marketing, when appropriate.
5. Organizational commitment to ethical Internet practices communicated to employees, customers, and relevant stakeholders.

They further assert that "Internet marketers must assess the risks and take responsibility for the consequences of their activities." (Houghton Mifflin Interactive 1998). They are warning advertisers to keep high ethical standards or risk very public criticism.

Many industries are taking these guidelines a step further and are trying to clarify the current laws and regulations in regard to the Internet. A good example of this is the law profession. As Professors Catherine Lanctot and James Maule at Villanova Unviersity Law School report "the state of the law...remains unsettled, and, as noted, the United States Supreme Court has recently signaled a willingness to permit greater state regulation of lawyer advertising...therefore, lawyers should assume that the advertising rules apply to any communications made on the Internet for the purpose of obtaining clients." (1998) They go on to suggest that solicitation regulations apply to a lawyer's homepage, direct e-mail, discussions that take place on-line, bulletin boards, Internet newsgroups, etc (1998).

The interests of privacy and growth of a new digital economy can be reconciled. Existing technology could allow customers to make electronic purchases while controlling the release of information about what they are saying. Although in the United States a law proposed by the Federal Bureau of Investigations (FBI) would mandate an electronic peephole in all encryption programs so that government agents can read all files in some other countries people are experimenting with solutions to some of these consumer concern. In Sweden, for example, where 40 percent of the population has Internet access, the following three issues have been tied to expanding e-commerce:

*   Consumers must be able to make secure payments, meaning that their funds cannot be stolen.
*   They must be able to send secure messages, meaning that their orders and preferences are not shared with others without their approval.
*   Secure logistics must be able to reliably deliver goods and services ordered on line (Sagan 1998: 47).

It is clear that at some point, government will ultimately need to address these issues on a broader basis. One of the questions this raises is "which government?" It goes beyond state versus federal regulation. The Internet is a worldwide medium. Eventually there will have to be a global regulating body to address ethical issues such as these.

Another concern is that of access. One of the benefits to advertisers is that the majority of Internet users are affluent. According to a survey conducted by Neilsen Research and CommerceNet in 1995, "on average, WWW users are upscale (25 percent have income over $80K), professional (50 percent are managerial or professional) and educated (64 percent have at least college degrees)." (Elbel 1998) As Karen Coyle stated in a seminar on the Ethics of the Internet, "there is very little commercial incentive to provide information to low income or minority segments of our society — the profit margin is just too low. So we are more likely to have information that benefits car owners than public transit users." (Advertising on the internet: The best marketing tool available! 1998). If the Internet is to become an economic and commercial force, there must be access for all segments of society. In the future, perhaps computers will be as common as televisions in every home, but affordability should be more of a concern as technological advances continue to speed through our society.

The last ethical issue to be addressed in this chapter is that of the human element. Since the first computers were introduced, there has been a fear that they would one day be able to think for themselves and eventually replace the more fragile human being. Computers have come a long way towards that, but are still nowhere near taking over, yet. They are, however, replacing the jobs of many humans. From travel agents, to car salespeople, to cashiers, the trend toward electronic interactive advertising is eliminating the need for human interaction. Even the advent of expert systems is eliminating the need for human experts. Computers are being programmed with the beliefs and perceptions of experts so that the machines may then emulate their decision making process to determine the most profitable course of action. Once the computer is fed the knowledge, it eliminates the need for the person.

The main predicament that these ethical issues indicate is that the Internet is so new, and so rapidly growing and changing, that society has not kept abreast of these questions. In order for public administrators to lead the people into the future, they must be aware of these issues. They must be able to address the needs and concerns of the people using these systems. They must also be ready to make difficult decisions regarding a future where physical boundaries become meaningless and the dissemination of information and communication become even more free than they are in the United States today.

The Internet as a market place has incredible potential if we can make sure it is used properly by all.

BIBLIOGRAPHY

Advertising on the internet. 1998. In Duke University [Web site]. North Carolina [cited 1998]. Available from http://www.duke.edu/~nmk/project.html; INTERNET.

Advertising on the Internet: The best marketing tool available! 1998. In Compunet Services, Inc. [Web site]. Douglasville, Georgia-[cited 1998]. Available from http://www.dla.vcop.edu/~kec/ethics.html; INTERNET.

African Development Bank. 1993. *African development report* 1993. Abidjan, Ivory Coast: ADB.

AltaVista. 1998. In AltaVista Search Engine [Web site]. [cited March 1998]. Available from http://www.altavista.com; INTERNET.

Amnesty International. 1993. Getting away with murder: *Political killings and "disappearances" in the 1990s*. New York: Amnesty International Publications.

Baker, R., ed. 1992. *Public administration in small and island states*. West Hartford, CT: Kumarian Press, Inc.

Barratt, J. and the South African Institute of International Affairs. 1976. *Strategy for development*. London: McMillan.

Barry, T. 1991. *Central America inside out*. New York: Grove Weindenfeld.

Beabout, G.R. and D. J. Wenneman. 1994. *Applied professional ethics: A developmental approach for use with case studies*. Lanham, Maryland: University Press of America.

Benedict, B. 1967. *Problems of smaller territories*. London: The Athlone Press.

Bennett, W.C., and B. B. Bird. 1949. *Andean culture history*. New York: Lancaster Press.

Berg, E. J. 1993. *Rethinking technical cooperation: Reforms for capacity building in Africa*. New York: United Nations Development Program.

Berman, P. B. 1980. Thinking about programmed and adaptive implementations: Matching strategies to situations. In *Why policies succeed or fail*, edited by H. M. Ingram and D. Mann. Beverly Hills: Sage.

Bigelow, P. E., ed. 1995. *International conference on ethics in government proceedings*. New York: The Institute of Public Administration.

Bond, E. J. 1996. *Ethics and human well being*. Cambridge, Massachusetts: Blackwell Publishers.

Booth, J.A. and M. A. Seligson, eds. 1989. *Elections and democracy in Central America*. Chapel Hill: University of North Carolina Press.

Borjas, G. J. and S. J. Trejo. 1991. Immigrant participation in the welfare system. *Industrial and Labor Relations Review* 44: 195-211.

Brinkerhoff, D. W. and A. A. Goldsmith. 1991. Sustainability of development institutions: A strategic framework. Presented at the annual meeting of the American Society for Public Administration, Washington, D.C.

Brumback, R. A. 1988. Teaching public administration in post-literate society. The political science teacher, (Spring).

Bryant, C. 1976. *Participation, planning, and administrative development in urban development programs*. Washington, D.C.: Agency for International Development.

Bryant, C. and L. G. White. 1982. *Managing development in the Third World*. Boulder, Colorado: Westview Press.

___. 1984. Managing rural development with small farmer participation. Hartford, CT: Kumarian Press.

Buchanan, S. H. 1980. *Haitian emigration*: The perspectives from South Florida and Haiti. Washington, D.C.: A Report submitted to the United States Agency for International Development (USAID).

Burland, C. and W. Forman. 1985. *The Aztecs: Gods and fate in ancient Mexico.* London: Orbis.

Caiden, G. E. 1970. *Israel's administrative culture.* Berkeley, CA.: University of California, Institute of Governmental Studies.

___. 1989. The Problem of Ensuring the Public Accountability of Public Officials. In *Public service accountability.* A comparative perspective, edited by J. G. Jabbra and O. P. Dwivedi. West Hartford, Connecticut: Kumarian Press.

Calvari, V. 1976. The world of the Maya. Geneva: Editions Minerva.

Cart, D. 1990. The impact of the Mariel boatlift on the Miami labor market. *Industrial and Labor Relations Review* 43: 245-257.

Cheena, S.G and D. A. Rondinelli, eds. 1983. *Decentralization and development.* Beverly Hills, California: Sage.

City of Miami. 1991. *The comprehensive housing affordability strategy.* Miami, Florida.

City of Miami, Department of Community Development. 1992. *Community development block grant program.* Miami, Florida.

___. 1993. *Community development status report.* 1st-18 Years. 1975-1993. Miami, Florida.

Coe, M. D. 1987. *The Maya.* New York: Thames & Hudson.

Cohen, R. 1980. The blessed job in Nigeria. In *Hierarchy and society: Anthropological perspectives on bureaucracy,* edited by Gerald M. Britan and Ronald Cohen. Philadelphia: Institute for the Study of Human Issues.

Crawley, R.W. 1965. The training of public servants. In *Public administration in developing Countries,* edited by M. Kriesberg. Washington, D.C.: The Brookings Institution.

Dade County Public Schools, Office of Educational Accountability. 1984. *District and school profiles,* 1983-84. Miami, Florida.

___. Office of Educational Accountability. 1992a. *District and school profiles,* 1991-92. Miami, Florida.

___. Office of Educational Accountability. 1992b. *Statistical abstract*, 1991-1992. Miami, Florida.

Davies, N. 1973. *The Aztecs: A history.* New York: G.P. Putnam's Sons.

de Smith, S. A. 1970. *Microstates and micronesia: Problems of America's Pacific Islands and other minute territories.* London: University of London Press, Ltd.

Denhardt, K. G. 1988. *The ethics of public service.* Westport, Connecticut: Greenwood Press.

Denhardt, R.B. 1995. *Public administration: An action orientation.* 2d ed. New York: Wadsworth Publishing Company.

Diaz, G.M., ed. 1985. *Report on the demographic characteristics of Mariel Cubans.* Miami, Florida: Cuban National Planning Council.

Dimock, M.E., G. O. Dimock, and D. M. Fox. 1983. *Public administration.* 5th ed. New York: Holt, Rinehart and Winston.

Dodge, D. 1966. *African politics in perspective.* New York: Van Nostrand.

Downs, A. 1994. *Inside bureaucracy.* Prospect Heights: Illinois: Waveland Press, Inc.

Dunham, R.G. and Werner, R.A. 1991. The trends and geography of crime in Metropolitan Dade County, Florida. In *South Florida: The wind of change,* edited by T. D. Boswell. Prepared for the Annual Conference of the Association of American Geographers.

Dwivedi, O.P. 1985. Ethics and values of public responsibility and accountability. *International Review of Administrative Science* LI, no.1.

Economic Intelligence Unit. 1992. Guatemala, El Salvador, Honduras. Parts 1 and 2. *EIU country report*, no. 3: 15-17; no. 4: 11-25.

Elbel, Fred. 1998. *Junk e-mail and spam: How to Get Rid of Junk Mail, Spam, and Telemarketers.* 1998. In EcoFuture [Web site]. 1998-[updated 7 February 1998; cited March 1998]. Available from http://www.ecofuture.org/ecofuture/jnkmail. html; INTERNET.

Electronic billboards on the digital superhighway: A Report of the Working Group on Internet Advertising. 1998. In The Coalition for Networked Information [Web site]. Washington, DC., 1994-[written 1994; cited March 1998]. Available from. http://www.cni.org/projects/advertising; INTERNET.

Elliot, J. M. and S. R. Ali. 1984. *The presidential congressional political dictionary.* Santa Barbara: ABC-CLIO Information Service.

Esman, M. J. 1974. Administrative doctrine and developmental needs. In *The administration of change in Africa,* edited by Philip Morgan. New York: Dunellen.

Fesler, J. W. and D. F. Kettl. 1996. *The politics of the administrative process.* 2d ed. Chatham, New Jersey: Chatham House Publishers, Inc.

First, R. 1970. *Power in Africa.* New York: Pantheon Books.

Fix, M. and J. S. Passel. 1991 *The door remains open: Recent immigration to the United States and a preliminary analysis of the Immigration Act of 1990.* Washington, D.C.: The Urban Institute.

Florida Department of Health and Rehabilitative Services, Refugee programs administration. 1992. *Florida's refugee fact book.* Tallahassee, Florida: HRS-OSRA.

Frederickson, H. G. 1993. *Ethics and public administration.* Armonk, New York: M.E. Sharpoe.

Gallagher, P. L. 1980. *The Cuban Exile. A Socio-Political Analysis.* New York, New York: Arno Press.

Gallenkamp, C. 1976. Maya: *The riddle and rediscovery of a lost civilization.* New York: David McKay Co.

Garcia-Zamor, J. C. 1976. Rumor as political communication in developing countries. *Administrative Change* 4: 68-73. Jaipur, India

____. 1977. *The ecology of development administration in Jamaica, Trinidad and Tobago, and Barbados.* Washington, D.C.: Organization of American States.

____. ed. 1978. *Politics and administration in Brazil.* Washington, D.C.: University Press of America.

___. ed. 1985. *Public participation in development planning and management: Cases from Africa and Asia.* Boulder, Colorado: Westview Press.

___. 1986. Obstacles to institutional development in Haiti. In *Politics, projects, and people: Institutional development in Haiti,* edited by D. W. Brinkerhoff and J. C. Garcia-Zamor. New York: Praeger Publishers.

___. 1987. Voluntary early retirement by Malian civil servants. *Administrative Change* 14, nos. 1-2, (July 1986-June 1987).

___. 1992. Voluntary early retirement by Malian civil servants. In *Administration for human resources: Comparative foci,* edited by R.K. and R. M Khandelwal. Jaipur, India: Arihant Publishers.

___. 1994. Neotenic theories for development administration in the new world order. In *Public administration in the global village,* edited by J. C. Garcia-Zamor and R. Khator. Westport, Ct.: Greenwood Publishers.

___. 1996. Obstacles to public policy implementation in the Third World. In *Advances in developmental policy studies,* edited by S. S. Nagel. Greenwich, Connecticut: JAI Press Inc.

___. 1997. The pitfalls of administrative reform in a ministate: The Case of Sao Tome and Principe. *21st Century Policy Review* 3, no. 3-4. (Fall-Winter): 79-100.

___. 1998. Administrative practices of the Aztecs, Incas, and Mayas: Lessons for modern administration. *International Journal of Public Administration* 1, no.1: 145-171.

Garfinkel, S. 1996. *PGP: Pretty good privacy.* Ingram Books.

Gaul, S. 1993 . *Malta, Gozo, and Comino.* London: Cadogen Books Ltd.

Geddes, Barbara. 1991. A game theoretic model of reform in Latin American democracies. *American Political Science Review* 85: 371-92.

Ghartey, J.B. 1986. *Consolidate accountability for development in Africa.* Boston: African Studies Center. Working Papers, no. 116.

___. 1987. Crisis accountability and development in the Third World. Brookfield, VA: Avebury.

Goldston, J.A. 1989. Shattered hope: Guatemalan workers and the promise of democracy. Boulder, Colorado: Westview Press.

Goodman, L. and R. Love. 1979. *Management of developing projects: An international case study approach.* Hawaii: Permagon Press.

Goodsell, C.T. 1994. *The case for bureaucracy: A public administration polemic.* 3rd ed. Chatham, New Jersey: Chatham House Publishers, Inc.

Gordon, G. J. 1986. *Public administration in America*, 3d ed. New York: St. Martin's Press.

Gortner, H. F. 1991. *Ethics for public managers.* Westport, Connecticut: Greenwood Press.

Gould, D. J. and J. A. Amaro-Reyes. 1983. *The effects of corruption on administrative performance: Illustrations from developing countries.* Washington D.C.: The World Bank.

Grenier, G. J. and A. Stepick, eds. 1992. Miami Now. Immigration, ethnicity, and social change. Gainesville, Florida: University of Florida Presses.

Harbeson, W. and D. Rothchild. 1995. *Africa in world politics: Post-cold war challenges.* Boulder, Colorado: Westview Press, Inc.

Hamilton, L. 1988. *Remarks on activity of foreign affairs.* Committee task force on foreign assistance. Washington, D.C., September 14, 1988.

Hammergreen, L. A. 1983. Development and the politics of administrative reform: Lessons from Latin America. Boulder, Colorado: Westview Press.

Handy, J. 1988. The most precious fruit of the revolution: The Guatemalan agrarian reform, 1952-54. *Hispanic American Historical Review* 68: 704-705.

Hann, J. H., ed. and trans. 1991. *Missions to the Calusa.* Gainesville, Florida: University of Florida Presses.

Hansen, A. and D. E. McMillan, eds. 1986. *Food in sub-Saharan Africa.* Boulder: Lynne Rienner.

Harris, R. L. 1965. The role of the civil servant in West Africa. *Public Administration Review* 25 (December): 309.

Hasenfeld, Y. 1985. Citizens' encounters with welfare state bureaucracies. Social Service Review 59: 622-635.

Heady, F. 1996. *Public administration: A comparative perspective.* 5th ed. New York: Marcel Dekker, Inc.

Henderson, J.S. 1981. *The world of the ancient Maya.* Ithaca, New York: Cornell University Press.

Hirschman, A. O. 1958. *The strategy of economic development.* New Haven: Yale University Press.

Hoagland, A.C. 1992. Reforming the revolution: Mexico influences the Ejido Liberates religion. *North-South: The Magazine of the Americas,* October-November, 38-41.

Honadle, G. and J. Vansant. 1985. *Implementation for sustainability: Lessons from integrated rural development.* West Hartford, CT.: Kumarian Press, Inc.

Hopkins J. W. 1967. *The government executives of modern Peru.* Gainesville, Florida: University of Florida Press.

Houghton Mifflin Interactive. 1998. In Houghton Mifflin Interactive [Web site]. Somerville, MA [cited 1998]. Available from http://www.hminet.com/hmco/college/PridFerr; INTERNET.

Hyams, E. and Ordish, G. 1963. *The last of the Incas: The rise and fall of an American empire.* New York: Simon & Schuster.

IBC International Country Risk Guide. 1991. May.

Institute of Public Opinion Research. 1992. *Florida poll.* Miami, FL: Florida International University.

Jain, R.B. 1989. Public service accountability in India. In *Public service accountability. A comparative perspective,* edited by Jabbra, J. G. and O. P. Dwivedi, O.P. West Hartford, Connecticut: Kumarian Press.

Jeffrey, P. 1991. Central America: Call it peace? *Christianity and Crisis* 52: 149-152.

Jones, C. O. 1984. *An introduction to the study of public policy*. 3d ed. Monterey, California: Cole.

Jreisat, J. E. 1988. Administrative reform in developing countries: A comparative perspective. *Public Administration and Development* 8: 85-97.

Karen, R. 1975. *The Inca: Empire builders of the Americas*. New York: Four Winds Press.

Kaufman, H. 1977. *Red tape: Its designs, uses and abuses*. Washington, D.C.: Brookings Institute.

Kennedy, P. 1994. *Preparing for the twenty-first century*. New York: Vintage Books.

Kenye, R. H. 1985. Politics, bureaucratic corruption and maladministration in Third World. *International Review of Administrative Science* L1, no. 1.

King, F. H. 1973. The foreign policy of Singapore. In The other powers:. *Studies in the foreign policies of small states*, edited by R. P. Barston. New York: Harper & Row Publishers, Inc.

Koenig, L. A. 1986. *An introduction to public policy*. Englewood Cliffs, N.J.: Prentice Hall.

Lagos, G. 1963. *International stratification and underdeveloped countries*. Chapel Hill, North Carolina: The University of North Carolina Press.

Lamouse-Smith, B. 1974. Complexity and African development administration: A sociological perspective. In *The Administration of change in Africa*, edited by P. Morgan. New York: Dunellen.

Lanctot C. J. and Maule J. E. 1998. *The internet — hip or hype? Legal ethics and the internet*. In Villanova University Law School [Web site]. Villanova, Pennsylvania [cited 1998]. Available from http://www.law.vill.edu/vcilp/ acCrate/ cle/lanctot.htm; INTERNET.

Lassey, W.R. and R. R. Fernandez, eds. 1976. *Leaders and social change*. San Diego: University Associates, Inc.

Lawrence, P., ed. 1986. *World recession and the food crisis in Africa*. London: James Curry Ltd.

Lee, D.S. 1990. Management theory and training. *Public Administration Quarterly* 14: 245-256.

Lui, T. T. 1994. Administrative ethics in a Chinese society: The case of Hong Kong. *In Handbook of administrative ethics*, edited by T. L. Cooper New York: Marcel Dekker, Inc.

Lyons, W.E., D.Lowery, and R. H. DeHoog, R.H. 1992. *The politics of dissatisfaction*. New York: M. E. Sharpe, Inc.

Magubane, B. and Nzongola-Ntalaja, eds. 1983. *Proletarianization and class struggle in Africa*. San Francisco: Synthesis Publications.

Martin, L. 1974. *The kingdom of the sun: A short history of Peru*. New York: Charles Scribner's Sons.

Masud-Piloto, F.R. 1988. *With open arms*: Cuban migration to the United States. Totowa, New Jersey: Rowman and Littlefield Publishers.

Mazmanian, D. A. and P. A. Sabatier. 1983. *Implementation and public policy*. Glenview, Ill.: Scott, Foresman and Company.

McCullough, H. 1994. Ethics Legislation. In *Handbook of administrative ethics*, edited by T.L. Cooper. New York: Marcel Dekker, Inc.

Means, P.G. 1964. *Fall of the Inca empire*. New York: Gardian Press, Inc.

Mende ,T. 1973. *From aid to recolonization: Lessons of a failure*. New York: Pantheon.

Menzel, D.C. 1997. Teaching ethics and values in public administration: Are we making a Difference? *Public Administration Review* 57: 224-230.

Metro-Dade Planning Department, Research Division. 1988. *Annual population report*. Miami, Florida.

Meyer, M.C. and W. L. Sherman. 1987. *The courses of Mexican history*. New York: Oxford University Press.

Moore, M. H. 1995. *Creating public value*. Cambridge, Massachusetts: Harvard University Press.

Moore, M.H. and M. K. Sparrow. 1990. *Ethics in government: The moral challenge of public Leadership*. Englewood Cliffs, New Jersey: Prentice-Hall.

Morley, S.G. and G. W. Brainerd. 1983. *The ancient Maya*. 4th ed. Revised by R. J. Sharer. Stanford, California: Stanford University Press.

Moyo, J.N. 1994. Administrative ethics in an African society: The case of Zimbabwe. In *Handbook of administrative ethics*, edited by T. L Cooper. New York: Marcel Dekker, Inc.

Munishi, G.K. 1989. Bureaucratic feudalism, accountability and development in the third world: The case of Tanzania. In *Public accountability: A Comparative Perspective*, edited by J.G. Jabbra. and O. P. Dwivedi. West Harford, Connecticut: Kumarian Press.

Muyoba, G.G. 1989. Accountability in the Zambian public service. In *Public service accountability: A comparative perspective*, edited by J. G. Jabbra and O. P. Dwivedi. West Harford, Connecticut: Kumarian Press.

National Association of Hispanic Public Administrators. 1991. *Towards parity: A report on Metropolitan Dade County's work* force. Miami, Florida.

Neuman, S. G. 1976. *Small states and segmented societies: National political integration in a global environment*. New York: Praeger Publishers.

Olowu, D. and V. Ayeni. 1989. Public service accountability in Nigeria. *In Public service accountability. A comparative perspective*, edited by J. G. Jabbra, J.G. and O. P. Dwivedi. West Hartford, Connecticut: Kumarian Press.

Peters, B. Guy. 1988. *Comparing public bureaucracies: Problems of theory and method*. Tuscaloosa, Alabama: The University of Alabama Press.

Peterson, F.A. 1979. *Ancient Mexico*. New York: A Paragon Book.

Piven, F. F.and A. C. Richard. 1988. *Why Americans don't vote*. New York: Pantheon Books.

Plano, J. C. and M. Greenberg. 1982. *The American political dictionary*. New York: Holt, Rinehart and Winston.

Pops, G. M. 1991. Improving ethical decision-making using the concept of justice. In *Ethical frontiers in public management*, edited by J. S. Bowman. San Francisco: Jossey-Bass Publishers.

Portney, K. E 1986. *Approaching public policy analysis: An introduction to policy and program research*. Englewood Cliffs, N.J.: Prentice-Hall.

Pressman, J. L. and A. Wildavsky. 1984. *Implementation*. 3d ed. Berkeley: University of California Press.

Price, R. M. 1975. *Society and bureaucracy in contemporary Ghana*. Berkeley, California: University of California Press.

Raadschelders, J.B. 1992. Definitions of smallness: A comparative study. In *Public administration in small and island states*, edited by R. Baker. West Hartford, Connecticut: Kumarian Press.

Reich, R. B. 1992. *The work of nations: Preparing ourselves for 21st-century capitalism*. New York: Vintage Books.

Riggs, F.W. 1964. *Administration in developing countries: The prismatic model*. *Boston*: Houghton Mifflin Company.

Rosen, B. 1982. Holding government bureaucracies accountable. New York: Praeger.

Rowat, Donald C. 1988. *Public administration in developed democracies: A Comparative Study*. New York: Marcel Dekker, Inc.

Sabine, C.D., ed. 1973. *Accountability: Systems planning in education*. Homewood, Ill: ETC Publications.

Sagan, P. 1998. The new buzz in IT. On-line commerce takes business by storm. Report on the 1998 Annual Meeting of the World Economic Forum: The View from Davos. Geneva, Switzerland.

Schydlowsky, D.M., ed. 1995. *Structural adjustment: Retrospect and prospect*. Westford, Connecticut: Praeger Publishers.

Scott, D. 1990. Anti-corruption plan gains ground in Mexico. *Christian Science Monitor* (18 December).

Sechrest, D.K. and P. Burns. 1992. Police corruption: The Miami case. *Criminal Justice and Behavior* 19: 294-313.

Sembor, E. and M. E. Leighninger. 1996. Rediscovering the public: Reconnecting ethics and ethos through democratic civic institutions. In *Ethical dilemmas in public administration*, edited by L. Pasquerella, A. G. Killilea, and M. Vocino. Westort, Connecticut: Praeger Publishers.

Serra, G. 1995. Citizen-initiated contact and satisfaction with bureaucracy: A multivariate analysis. *Journal of Public Administration Research and Theory* 5: 175-188.

Sheeran, P. J. 1993. *Ethics in public administration.* Westport. Connecticut: Praeger Publishers.

Smith, T.E. 1967. Demographic Aspects of Smallness. In *Problems of smaller territories*, edited by B. Benedict. London: The Athlone Press.

Smith, G.E. and C. A. Huntsman. 1997. Reframing the metaphor of the citizen-government relationship: A value-centered perspective. *Public Administration Review*, 57: 309-318.

Stepick, A. 1992. The refugees nobody wants: Haitians in Miami. In *Miami Now: Immigration, ethnicity, and social change*, edited by G. J. Grenier and A. Stepick. Gainesville, Florida: University of Florida Presses.

Stepick, A. and C. D. Stepick. 1990. People in the shadows: Survey research among Haitians in Miami. *Human Organization* 49: 64-73.

Stogdill, R.M. 1981. *Stogdill's handbook of leadership.* New York: Free Press.

Stone, D. and A. Stone. 1976. Creation of administrative capacity: The missing ingredient in development strategy. In *Strategy for development*, edited by J. Barratt and the South African Institute of International Affairs. London: McMillian.

SuperNet. 1998. In SuperNet [Web site]. [cited March 1998]. Available from http://www.csnet.com/whatinet.htlm; INTERNET.

Terrell, K. 1989. Analysis of the wage structure in Guatemala City. *The Journal of Developing Areas* 23: 419-420.

Thompson, D. F. 1987. *Political ethics and public office*. Cambridge, Massachusetts: Harvard University Press.

Uchendu, V.C. 1976. Motivation and incentive structure for planned rural development. In *Strategy for development*, edited by J. Barratt and the South African Institute of International Affairs. London: McMillan.

United Nations Development Program and Development Alternatives, Inc. 1993. Rethinking technical cooperation. *Reforms for capacity building in Africa*. Coordinator: Elliot J. Berg. New York: UNDP.

United Nations Development Program (UNDP). 1993. *Human development report 1993*. New York: Oxford University Press.

____. 1995. *Human development report 1995*. New York: Oxford University Press.

United States Committee for Refugees. 1991 and 1992. *Refugee reports*. Washington, D.C.: U.S. Committee for Refugees.

Vasuki, S. N. 1998. The lions are coming. Will Africa become the next economic miracle. Report on the 1998 Annual Meeting of the World Economic Forum: The View from Davos. Geneva, Switzerland.

Vega, G. 1961. *The Inca: The royal commentaries of the Incas*. New York: The Orion Press.

Whitlock, R. 1976. *Everyday life of the Maya*. New York: G. P. Putnam's Sons.

World Almanac and Book of Facts. 1993. New York: Pharos Books.

World Bank. 1984. *Towards sustained development in sub-Saharan Africa: A joint program of action*. Washington, DC: The World Bank.

____. 1986. *The World Bank annual report*. Washington, D.C.: The World Bank.

____. 1993. *World development report 1993: Investing in health. World development indicators*. New York: Oxford University Press.

____. 1995. *World development report 1995*. New York: Oxford University Press.

SUBJECT INDEX

AUTHOR INDEX

ABOUT THE AUTHOR

Jean-Claude Garcia-Zamor is presently a tenured Professor of Public Administration in the School of Policy and Management of the College of Health and Urban Affairs at Florida International University (FIU). He joined FIU in 1990. He is also currently an Adjunct Professor of Ethics and Management at Leipzig University in the former East Germany where he teaches during the summer months. He has been teaching at Leipzig since the 1999 summer. From 1980 to 1989 he was a Professor of Public Policy and Administration in the Department of Political Science at Howard University. Previously, he taught in the Department of Government of the University of Texas at Austin and at the Brazilian School of Public Administration of the Getulio Vargas Foundation in Rio de Janeiro, Brazil. He has also lectured at the Venezuelan National School of Public Administration in Caracas, Venezuela; the United States Air Force Academy in Colorado Springs; the Catholic University of Argentina in Mendoza, Argentina; the University of Pittsburgh; the American University in Washington, D.C.; the Foreign Service Institute of the U.S. Department of State; the University of Idaho in Moscow, Idaho; the Canadian National School of Public Administration in Montreal and Quebec City; and both Delhi and Madras University in India. He has also visited all the countries of Latin America, the majority of the countries of the Caribbean, Africa, and Europe, New Zealand, Australia, India, South Korea, Thailand, and the People's Republic of China.

From 1971 to 1975, Dr. Garcia-Zamor was a Senior Specialist in Public Administration at the Organization of American States and from 1975 to 1977, he was President of the International Development Group, Inc., a Washington, D.C.-based consulting firm with twenty-five Associates. In 1977, he was elected by the Board of Directors of the Inter-American Development Bank to a two-year term to join the Board as Controller. He has done extensive consulting work in Latin America and Africa for the World Bank, the United Nations Development Program (UNDP), the Food and Agricultural Organization of the U.N. (FAO), the United States Agency for International Development (USAID), the Pan American Development Foundation, the National Institute of Public Management and several U. S. universities.

Dr. Garcia-Zamor is the author of four books: *La adminstración Pública en Haiti, Public Administration and Social Changes in Argentina: 1943-1955, The Ecology of Development in Trinidad and Tobago, Jamaica, and Barbados,* and *Administrative Ethics and Development Administration.* He is the editor of two books: *Politics and Administration in Brazil,* and *Public Participation for Development Administration: Cases from Africa and Asia.* He also co-edited three other books: *The Financing of Development in Latin America, Politics, Projects, and Peasants: Institutional Development in Haiti,* and *Public Administration in the Global Village.* He is also the author of many chapters in edited volumes and of numerous articles that have appeared in professional journals in the United States, Puerto Rico, Brazil, Belgium, Great Britain, the Netherlands, India, and China.

Dr. Garcia-Zamor holds a Master in Latin American History and a Ph.D. in Public Administration from New York University. He also holds a Master of Public Administration and a B.A. in Political Science from the University of Puerto Rico. He is a life member of the American Society for Public Administration and a member of several other professional organizations both in the U.S. and abroad.